GRAMMAR AND BEYOND

WORKBOOK

Kathryn O'Dell

3B

CAMBRIDGE
UNIVERSITY PRESS

CAMBRIDGE
UNIVERSITY PRESS

32 Avenue of the Americas, New York, NY 10013-2473, USA

Cambridge University Press is part of the University of Cambridge.

It furthers the University's mission by disseminating knowledge in the pursuit of education, learning and research at the highest international levels of excellence.

www.cambridge.org
Information on this title: www.cambridge.org/ 9781107601994

First published 2012
2nd printing 2014

Printed in the United States of America

A catalog record for this publication is available from the British Library.

ISBN 978-0-521-14296-0 Student's Book 2
ISBN 978-0-521-14310-3 Student's Book 2A
ISBN 978-0-521-14312-7 Student's Book 2B
ISBN 978-0-521-27991-8 Workbook 2
ISBN 978-0-521-27992-5 Workbook 2A
ISBN 978-0-521-27993-2 Workbook 2B
ISBN 978-1-107-67653-4 Teacher Support Resource with CD-ROM 2
ISBN 978-0-521-14335-6 Class Audio CD 2
ISBN 978-1-139-06186-5 Writing Skills Interactive 2

Art direction and layout services: Integra

Contents

PART 9 The Passive

PART 10 Relative Clauses (Adjective Clauses)

PART 11 Conditionals

PART 12 Connecting Ideas

UNIT 14

Negative Questions and Tag Questions

Geographic Mobility

Negative Questions

1 Complete the conversation with the negative question forms of the verbs in parentheses. Read the answers to the questions to help you with the verb forms.

Dan: Hey, Ben. What are you doing?

Ben: I'm reading research on geographic mobility in 2010. It's for my government class.

Dan: Oh . . . I read a few articles about this last semester. _Didn't_ a lot of people in the
(1)

United States _move_ (move) in 2010?
(1)

Ben: No, not really. Only 12.5 percent of the people in the United States moved.

Dan: Interesting. In general, _____ a lot of people _____
(2)   (2)

(move) to better homes?

Ben: Yes, almost half of the people who moved in 2010 did it for housing reasons.

Dan: What about other reasons? _____ people also _____
(3)   (3)

(change) cities in 2010 because of jobs?

Ben: Yes. A little more than 16 percent of the people who moved did so for work.

Dan: OK, but _____ (be) there other reasons for moving, too?
(4)

Ben: Yes, there are. People often move because of changes in their family situations.

Dan: I heard that people don't usually move far. _____ people often
(5)

_____ (stay) in the same area when they move?
(5)

Ben: Sure. In 2010, about 82 percent of the people who moved stayed in the same state.

Dan: Are the statistics only about people who moved within the United States?

_____ they _____ (include) people who moved to the
(6)   (6)

United States from other countries in 2010?

Ben: Of course they do. In total, about 3.5 percent of the people who moved came to the

United States from foreign countries.

2 Mr. Evans, a school principal, is speaking with Sofia on the phone about a teaching job. He doesn't have her résumé with him and can't remember all the information in it. Write negative questions with the words in parentheses. Then complete Sofia's answers with the information in her résumé.

Sofia Alba

Work

2008–Present   Dylan High School   Chicago, Illinois
English Teacher

2006–2008   North American School   Mexico City, Mexico
English Teacher

Education

2005   Martinson College   New York, New York
B.A., Education

Other Languages

Spanish and French

1. (graduate / from Martinson College)

   Mr. Evans: *Didn't you graduate from Martinson College?*

   Sofia: *Yes* , that's right. I graduated in *2005* .

2. (have / a degree in economics)

   Mr. Evans: _____

   Sofia: _____ . Actually, I have a degree in _____ .

3. (work / at Dyett High School now)

   Mr. Evans: _____

   Sofia: Actually, _____ . I work at _____ .

4. (live / in Chicago since 2006)

   Mr. Evans: _____

   Sofia: _____ . Actually, I've lived here since _____ .

5. (move / to Mexico City)

   Mr. Evans: _____

   Sofia: _____ , that's right. I moved there in _____ .

6. (speak / Spanish and Portuguese)

   Mr. Evans: _____

   Sofia: Well, actually, I speak _____ .

Tag Questions

1 Complete the questions. Circle the correct tags.

1. In the past, large companies were in big cities, **are they / aren't they / were they / ~~weren't they~~**?

2. Now, some companies are moving to smaller cities, **are they / aren't they / is it / isn't it**?

3. It can be cheaper to run a big company in a small city, **is it / isn't it / can it / can't it**?

4. That's not always true, **is it / isn't it / is that / isn't that**?

5. Everybody relocates when a company moves, **do they / don't they / does it / doesn't it**?

6. The owners of our company are deciding whether or not to move our company to a smaller town, **are they / aren't they / do they / don't they**?

7. Our boss hasn't told us the decision yet, **did he / didn't he / has he / hasn't he**?

8. There hasn't been a memo about it, **is there / isn't there / has there / hasn't there**?

9. Some employees won't be happy, **are we / aren't we / will they / do they**?

10. You wouldn't like to relocate, **did it / didn't it / would you / wouldn't you**?

2 Read the article from an alumni magazine. Complete the statements and tag questions. Then write the answers using the information in the article. Write the correct information after the *No* answers. Sometimes more than one answer is possible.

The Class of 2011

What are they doing now?

Here are the people from the Class of 2011 who have made the biggest changes:

1. Rajat Singh is working at a hospital in Dallas.

2. Jorge and Marta Baeza moved to Miami to start a family.

3. Brandon Harris is painting houses for his brother's company.

4. Olga Galdin moved to London to look for work.

5. Ali and Chuck Trenton bought a restaurant near the college.

6. Isabela Fuentes is living in Houston and teaching English.

1. **A:** Rajat _is working_ at a school, _isn't he_ ?

   B: _No, he isn't. He's working at a hospital._

2. **A:** Jorge and Marta _____ to Miami, _____ ?

   B: _____

3. **A:** Brandon _____ cars, _____ ?

   B: _____

4. **A:** Olga _____ to Lima, _____ ?

   B: _____

5. **A:** Ali and Chuck _____ a clothing store, _____ ?

   B: _____

6. **A:** Isabela _____ in Houston, _____ ?

   B: _____

3 Read the questions. Then circle the statements that describe what the speaker thinks. Use the intonation arrows to help you.

1. Jen and Marc are living in Alaska, aren't they?

   a. The speaker is not certain this statement is true.

   b. The speaker expects the listener to agree.

2. They moved there to find jobs, didn't they?

   a. The speaker is not certain this statement is true.

   b. The speaker expects the listener to agree.

3. Jen loves cold weather, doesn't she?

   a. The speaker is not certain this statement is true.

   b. The speaker expects the listener to agree.

4. But Marc doesn't like the cold, does he?

   a. The speaker is not certain this statement is true.

   b. The speaker expects the listener to agree.

5. They aren't coming home for the holidays, are they?

   a. The speaker is not certain this statement is true.

   b. The speaker expects the listener to agree.

4 A Complete the excerpts from the conversation with *Yes* or *No* short answers.

1. **Jake:** You saw the movie *Winged Migration*, didn't you?

   Diego: <u>Yes, I did</u> . It was great.

2. **Jake:** It's about birds migrating, isn't it?

   Diego: _____ . It shows

   them moving because of weather.

3. **Jake:** They didn't film it in one year, did they?

   Diego: _____ . It took over four years.

4. **Jake:** They filmed some of it in the United States, didn't they?

   Diego: _____ . However, they also filmed scenes in

   Iceland, Japan, and other countries.

5. **Jake:** It's available on DVD now, isn't it?

   Diego: _____ . Why don't you get it from the library?

B Look at the intonation arrows in the conversation in A. For each of Jake's questions, write *U* if he is uncertain of the information or *A* if he expects agreement from Diego.

1. <u>U</u>   2. _____   3. _____   4. _____   5. _____

5 Answer the questions with your own opinion. Use *yes* or *no*, and add one sentence with more information.

1. You would move for a job, wouldn't you?

   _____

2. You didn't move last year, did you?

   _____

3. You won't study another foreign language, will you?

   _____

4. You don't like cold weather, do you?

   _____

5. You enjoy your studies, don't you?

   _____

Avoid Common Mistakes

1 Circle the mistakes.

1. Vivian moved to Japan, **didn't she**? You're visiting her next month, **no** ? You're going
    (a) (b)

   with your sister, **aren't you**?
    (c)

2. **A: Isn't the company moving** the main office to a different location soon?
    (a)

   Aren't the managers supposed to tell us 60 days before the move?
    (b)

   B: Yes, they are. **You no get** the e-mail about it last week?
    (c)

3. **A: Didn't you** hear that Tom got a new job?
    (a)

   B: No, I didn't. I'm glad you told me. I guess his income will be higher now, **isn't he**?
    (b) (c)

4. **A:** He'll make a lot more money, and he'll also have to travel a lot. **Isn't it** great?
    (a)

   Wouldn't you like to have a job like his?
    (b)

   B: No. I'd love to travel for work.
    (c)

5. Julia's making a movie about why people move, **doesn't she**? It's for her film class,
    (a)

   isn't it? You'll go see it, **won't you**?
    (b) (c)

6. You can help me, **no**? You're moving to Toronto, **aren't you**? You can take this package
    (a) (b)

   to my brother, **can't you**?
    (c)

7. **A: Aren't you** working from home now?
    (a)

   B: Yes. My apartment is too small, so I still go to the office every day. **Don't you** agree
    (b) (c)

   it's better not to work at home?

8. **A: Isn't Zack helping** his parents move? **They no moving** to Florida?
    (a) (b)

   B: Yes, they are, but I don't think Zack is helping them. I think he's on vacation in Hawaii
    (c)

   right now.

2 Find and correct eight more mistakes in the interview with a doctor who works at a mobile health clinic.[1]

A Moving Doctor

Dr. Morris works for a mobile health clinic in Kenya. We interviewed him last week.

Q: You travel from place to place in Kenya, ~~doesn't he~~ *don't you*?

A: No. I travel a lot. I move from place to place with other doctors and nurses.

Q: You no working mostly in small towns?

5 **A:** Yes, I am. There aren't many hospitals there. We have a small hospital in a van.

Q: You drive the van from place to place, no?

A: Well, I don't drive it myself. Someone else drives it. We usually stay in a place for

a few weeks. Then we go to another town.

Q: This medical program helps a lot of people, doesn't she?

10 **A:** Yes, it does. We give health care to many people in small towns.

Q: You no get tired of moving around so much?

A: Yes. I never get tired. I love it.

Q: New doctors will be coming to your program next week, no?

A: Yes, they will. I'm going to be training six new doctors.

15 **Q:** Then you're going home, isn't it?

A: No, I'm not. Actually, I'm going to Ethiopia to set up a mobile clinic there.

---

[1]**mobile health clinic:** a doctor's office, usually in a van, that travels from place to place

Self-Assessment

Circle the word or phrase that correctly completes each sentence.

1. _____ you work for a moving company?

   a. Not do   b. Do not   c. Don't

2. Was Danilo _____ living in Seoul last year?

   a. not   b. no   c. wasn't

3. I'm so upset that I didn't get that job! _____ the best person to work in our office in Brazil?

    a. I'm not   b. Am not I   c. Aren't I

4. Hey, that woman looks like Liz. Didn't she _____ overseas?

    a. move   b. moved   c. not

5. **A:** Hasn't Yolanda moved to Florida? **B:** _____ . She moved to Miami, in southern Florida.

    a. No.   b. Yes, she has   c. No, she hasn't

6. They moved to a big city, _____ ?

    a. don't they   b. did they   c. didn't they

7. You're not from Argentina, _____ ?

    a. aren't you   b. are you   c. do you

8. You haven't lived in Asia, _____ ?

    a. did you   b. haven't you   c. have you

9. They were packing boxes, _____ ?

    a. weren't they   b. were they   c. didn't they

10. The students are studying migration trends, _____ ?

    a. aren't we   b. isn't it   c. aren't they

11. _____ a great place to live, isn't it?

    a. That's   b. Something's   c. Everyone's

12. Everyone has some issues with moving, _____ ?

    a. doesn't he   b. doesn't it   c. don't they

13. **A:** Tom moved when he got married, didn't he? **B:** _____ .

    a. Yes, he didn't   b. Yes, he did   c. No, he did

14. **A:** Your neighbors didn't move to New York City, did they? **B:** _____ . They moved to L.A.

    a. No, they didn't   b. Yes, they didn't   c. No, they did

15. **A:** You aren't driving to Seattle, are you? **B:** _____ . I can't afford to fly.

    a. Yes, I have to   b. No, I'm not   c. No, I don't

That Clauses

Cultural Values

That Clauses

1 Add *that* to five more noun clauses in the article.

Jobs with Values

Many jobs have different values associated with them. Here are just a few:

Doctors: Doctors value each patient's life. They even take an oath.[1] The oath
         that
says ∧ doctors must treat sick people to the best of their ability.

Doctors also promise to keep a patient's information private.

5   **Lawyers:** Privacy is also important in law. Lawyers know they cannot share a

client's information with others if the client doesn't want them to.

Lawyers also value fairness.

Teachers: Teachers value learning. They believe all students can learn.

Dentists: Dentists value good dental care. They know their patients will have

10   healthier teeth if they brush and floss them every day and see a

dentist regularly.

Librarians: Librarians value reading. They also think people should be quiet in

libraries to let other people concentrate on what they are reading.

Journalists: Journalists care about the truth. They learn they must be correct and

15   fair when reporting.

[1]**oath:** an official promise that you will do something

2 Read the sentences about how different cultures value time. Then rewrite each pair of sentences in bold as a single sentence with a noun clause. Omit *that* for the informal sentences.

1. Dr. Kim is an anthropologist. **He discovered something early in his career: People from different cultures value time differently.**

   Dr. Kim discovered that people from different cultures value time differently.
   (formal)

2. Paul is going to study in Brazil. **He assumes something: Brazilians don't usually mind being late for parties with close friends.**

   _____
   (informal)

3. Mr. Ito is researching German culture. **He has read something: Germans usually like to be on time.**

   _____
   (formal)

4. Melissa is visiting a friend in the United States. **She feels something: Americans are sometimes too worried about time.**

   _____
   (informal)

5. Ms. Piper is researching Canadian work habits. **She has noticed something: Canadians usually start meetings on time.**

   _____
   (formal)

6. Carolina is on vacation in Italy. **She has realized something: Sometimes it's not important to be on time in Italy.**

   _____
   (informal)

7. Dr. Robins is an architect, working on a project in China. **He understands something: Chinese people often plan things years in advance.**

   _____
   (formal)

8. Ben is staying in Tokyo. A Japanese friend invited him to a party. **He guesses something: People aren't often late for parties in Japan.**

   _____
   (informal)

3 Complete the sentences about time. Use *that* clauses. Write sentences that are true for you.

1. I think _that it's important to be on time for dinner at a friend's house_____.
                                 (dinner at a friend's house)

2. I've learned _____.
                                 (business meetings)

3. I've decided _____.
                                 (English class)

4. I understand _____.
                                 (a flight)

5. I believe _____.
                                 (birthday parties)

Agreement Between *That* Clauses and Main Clauses

1 Unscramble the sentences. Use the simple present form of the verbs in the main clause. Put the verbs in the *that* clause in the present, future, or past, as indicated in parentheses. Sometimes more than one answer is possible.

1. respect / say / experts / a common value in most cultures / that / be / (present)

   _Experts say that respect is a common value in most cultures._____

2. that / their parents / show / respect / research / most people / (present)

   _____

3. most parents / that / imagine / them / always respect / their children / (future)

   _____

4. deserve / learn / that / most children / grandparents / respect / (present)

   _____

5. people / feel / some historians / show others / that / more respect in the past / (past)

   _____

6. children / think / some teachers / that / be / more respectful in the past / (past)

   _____

7. students / some teachers / that / assume / listen better in the future / (future)

   _____

8. trends / experts / that / realize / change / over time / (future)

   _____

2 Complete the blog entry. Circle the correct form of the verbs. Use the information in parentheses and the explanations in the box to help you.

---

after = The event in the *that* clause happened after the event in the main clause.

before = The event in the *that* clause happened before the event in the main clause.

same = The event in the *that* clause happened at the same time as the event in the main clause.

truth = The *that* clause expresses a universal truth or fact that applies to the present.

I traveled a lot for work last year. I discovered that people **had valued /(value)**
(1. truth)
personal space differently in different parts of the world. For example, because

I'm Canadian, I know that Canadians **had stood / stand** about three feet apart
(2. truth)
when they talk. After a party at work in Quebec, however, I realized that

people there **had been standing / were going to stand** very close together.
(3. before)
I asked someone I work with about what I had noticed, and I found out that

French-speaking Canadians usually **had liked / like** to stand much closer
(4. truth)
than English-speaking Canadians.

Before I went to Japan, I had looked at some pictures of Tokyo online. I

noticed that people **are / were** generally close together on the streets and in
(5. same)
the subway, so I guessed that I **saw / would see** people very close together
(6. after)
everywhere in Japan. When I was there, though, I realized that people

didn't stand / doesn't stand close together at meetings and social events. I
(7. same)
found out that they **are / had been** usually close together on subways and in the
(8. truth)
streets because it is crowded in those places.

I hope that I won't be traveling as much next year. I want my own personal

space and would like to just stay home for a while. Nonetheless, I've learned

something about different cultures and personal space this year.

That Clauses After Adjectives and Nouns

1 Read the online comments about learning languages. Underline each adjective before a *that* clause. Circle each noun before a *that* clause.

Different cultures have different views on learning languages. What do you think about learning languages?

JL22: People in the United States often know only one language, but it's clear that people in Europe usually learn more than one language.

5 **KyleK:** It's understandable that Europeans know many languages. The countries are close together, and they need to communicate with each other.

DougT: It's unfortunate that people in the United States don't speak more languages. It's my view that there are many benefits to being bilingual![1]

10 **Mary96:** It is evident that bilingual people have advantages. It's understandable that bilingual people get better jobs.

Sandra: The problem is that not many schools in the United States offer enough foreign language classes.

George06: I disagree. My impression is that schools offer classes, but it's very
15 challenging to find places to speak other languages outside of class.

JavierR: I'm certain that people in my country value language learning. Almost everyone learns Spanish and English in school.

L1990: My hope is that everyone will speak both Spanish and English in the next 20 years.

20 **Mei92:** My concern is that people will still only be bilingual. It's fortunate that we speak three languages in my family.

Isabel: In some places there's a belief that learning only one language is the best. I guess the point is that a lot of us disagree!

---

[1] **bilingual:** able to speak two languages

2 Write sentences with *that* clauses. Use *It is* or *The . . . is* in the main clauses.

1. understandable / different cultures have different values

   It is understandable that different cultures have different values.

2. clear / different cultural values should be respected

   _____

3. problem / something considered positive by one culture might be considered negative by another

   _____

4. interesting / the Internet might help reduce these problems by making people more aware of other cultures

   _____

5. hope / people will learn more about cultural values in other countries

   _____

6. likely / there will be fewer conflicts because of different cultural values in the future

   _____

3 Complete the sentences with *that* clauses. Use the topics in the box or your own ideas. Write sentences that are true for you.

family life	personal relationships	speaking two languages	work
money	privacy	traditions	values

1. I think it's surprising _____ .

2. I am certain _____ .

3. I have the impression _____ .

4. My concern is _____ .

5. It is my belief _____ .

6. I find it unfortunate _____ .

7. I think it's interesting _____ .

Avoid Common Mistakes

1 Circle the mistakes.

1. (John recognized, that) cultural values were different in Mexico than they were in his
(a)
country. **He realized that** people viewed time differently. He found out **he was** able to
(b)   (c)
adapt easily.

2. It's disappointing **that Chinese classes aren't** available at our school. I'm not sure
(a)
that people value learning other languages enough. I hope **that more language classes be**
(b)   (c)
available in the future.

3. It's embarrassing **that don't speak Spanish better**. I realize **that it's important** to speak
(a)   (b)
other languages. It's true **that I've been trying**, but it's difficult for me.
(c)

4. **Research shows that** values differ in different cultures. **Experts do not believe, that**
(a)   (b)
one culture is right and another is wrong. **They think that** it is important to understand
(c)
the differences.

5. Diana and Jim realize **that they should respect** their parents. Their parents are relieved
(a)
that their children understand this value as well. They feel lucky **that have** respectful
(b)   (c)
children.

6. Tom **understands that culture** influences **values, but** he's **not sure, that his values**
(a)   (b)   (c)
are influenced by culture.

7. Many cultures believe **that hard work is** important. Research shows **that this idea is**
(a)   (b)
usually true in these cultures – people who work harder are usually more successful and

happier. According to psychologists, it is not surprising **that parents teaching** their
(c)
children this value.

8. I'm glad **that I'm learning** about different cultures. I'm surprised **that I learning** so
(a)   (b)
much in this class. I'm disappointed **that the class is going to end** soon.
(c)

2 Find and correct seven more mistakes in the article about diverse cities.

Diverse Cities in the World

    There are many places in the world that are culturally diverse. It is interesting ∧*that* people

with different cultural values can often get along well in these places. Here are some of

the most diverse cities in the world.

    New York City: It is clear that New York City always been culturally diverse. People

5 speak around 800 languages in the city. Immigrants have come to New York City from all

over the world, and experts are certain that the trend continue in the future.

    Toronto: Toronto is Canada's most diverse city. It is true, that French and English are

official languages in Canada, but research shows that almost one-third of the people in

Toronto speak a foreign language at home. Over half of the people living in Toronto were

10 not born in Canada.

    Los Angeles: Los Angeles is another diverse city. Research shows, that almost half of

the population is Latino, 14 percent is Asian, and 9 percent is African American. L.A.

is diverse in other ways, too. Experts say that is the creative capital of the world.

    London: One website says that, almost every culture in the world can be found in

15 London. The large number of cultures is reflected in the restaurants, in which you can

find a variety of food from around the world.

    Dubai: Dubai is quickly becoming a diverse city. It is surprising that was not diverse

in the past. Many people from around the world have moved there for work, making it a

global city today.

Self-Assessment

Circle the word or phrase that correctly completes each sentence.

1. This book says _____ affects the way we think.

   a. that   b. that culture   c. is

2. Briana _____ all journalists should tell the truth.

   a. believes, that   b. believes that,   c. believes that

3. Doctors take an oath that says they _____ all patients to the best of their ability.

   a. treated   b. will treat   c. have treated

4. Do you _____ that people have different values?

   a. understand   b. show   c. have

5. Many Americans feel that individualism _____ extremely important today.

   a. not be   b. is   c. was

6. Historians recognize that people _____ hard to survive in the past.

   a. work   b. are working   c. worked

7. I have decided that I _____ Japanese next year.

   a. will study   b. study   c. have studied

8. My parents knew that I _____ respectful to my teachers at the meeting yesterday.

   a. was   b. am   c. will be

9. The study showed that most teenagers _____ their grandparents.

   a. are going to respect   b. respect   c. will respect

10. Ms. Lang found out that her students _____ the homework on values. They had to do it together in class.

    a. aren't completing   b. hadn't completed   c. won't complete

11. I heard that Dr. Roberts _____ his books at the new bookstore.

    a. selling   b. would selling   c. would be selling

12. It's _____ that I won't understand the culture in a country whose language I don't speak.

    a. likely   b. unlikely   c. fortunate

13. _____ clear that Erica loves to learn about other cultures.

     a. It's   b. It   c. She

14. It was our _____ that Rich wouldn't move to another country.

     a. possibility   b. difference   c. impression

15. The _____ is that no one understands us.

     a. problem   b. views   c. frightening

Noun Clauses with *Wh-* Words and *If/Whether*

Inventions They Said Would Never Work

Noun Clauses with *Wh-* Words

1 Complete the excerpts from a conversation about Thomas Edison. Use *how, how many, what, when, where, which, who,* or *why.*

1. **A:** I can't remember <u>when</u> Thomas Edison was born.

   B: He was born in 1847.

2. **A:** I don't know _____ Edison was born.

   B: He was born in Ohio in the United States.

3. **A:** I wonder _____ brothers and sisters Edison had.

   B: He had six brothers and sisters.

   A: Do you know _____ was the youngest?

   B: He was!

4. **A:** I wonder _____ Edison became interested in science.

   B: I know he was just a child. Edison always wanted to figure out _____ things worked.

5. **A:** I'd like to know _____ Edison didn't talk until he was four years old. What was the reason?

   B: I don't know, but I do know this . . . when he started to talk, he was always asking questions!

6. **A:** I'd like to know _____ new things Thomas Edison invented.

   B: I don't know for sure, but he had over 1,000 patents.

7. **A:** I know _____ invention was Edison's most famous!

   B: I know that one, too – the light bulb!

8. **A:** Did you know that Thomas Edison had substantial hearing loss by age 12?

   B: I don't know _____ caused his hearing loss.

   A: Experts have different opinions on the cause. Regardless, Edison became one of the most important inventors in U.S. history.

2 Complete the article with *how, what, when,* or *where* and the words in parentheses. Use the simple present or infinitive form of the verbs. Sometimes more than one answer is possible.

<u>*What is*</u> (be) amazing about online shopping is that in 1966, *Time* magazine said it
(1)
would never work! Most people today are comfortable with online shopping, but there are

some things you should consider when you buy items online.

- You have to understand _____ (expect) as extra costs. Most
(2)
  companies charge money for shipping.[1] Depending on _____
(3)
  (the item / come) from and _____ (you / want) it, this can get
(4)
  expensive.

- It's important to remember that _____ (you / see)
(5)
  isn't always _____ (you / get). You need to learn
(6)
  _____ (look) for important details in the photographs and descriptions
(7)
  of products. Even when you do this, there are sometimes surprises when the item arrives.

- Finally, it's a good idea to know _____ (find) reviews of products.
(8)
  It can be very helpful to see _____ (people / say) about products.
(9)

[1]**shipping:** the act of sending something to a customer

3 Unscramble the sentences about an alternative fuel.

1. are trying / how / algae[1] into fuel / to turn / researchers / to figure out

   <u>*Researchers are trying to figure out how to turn algae into fuel.*</u>

2. can be used in cars / they / when / the "algae fuel" / still don't know

   _____

3. with the research / what / happens / many people / care about

   _____

4. may affect / of the project / the results / we power our cars in the future / how

   _____

5. will happen / I'm / not sure / what / with this new technology

   _____

6. however, I / why / can understand / are interested in it / so many people

   _____

[1]**alga:** (plural *algae*) a type of plant that grows in water

Noun Clauses with *If / Whether*

1 Complete the conversation. Use the questions in the box to complete the noun clauses with *if / whether*.

> Is Sandwich the name of a place?
> Did it happen in the 17th or 18th century?
> Did the earl like his sandwich?
> Did the sandwich become popular right away?
> ~~Did you read the article on the naming of the sandwich?~~
> Is the place in England or North America?
> Was the name from the servant who prepared it or from the man who ate it?

Ms. Moore: OK, class. Let's talk about the homework. I'd like to know whether or not

   you read the article on the naming of the sandwich .
   (1)

   Dan, where did the sandwich get its name?

Dan: Well, I don't remember whether _____
   (2)

   _____ .

Yuko: I remember! It was from the man who ate it. The story is that the fourth Earl of

   Sandwich was playing a card game, and he wanted to eat while he played. His

   servant put some meat between two pieces of bread so that the Earl could eat

   quickly and not stop playing. So the sandwich got its name from the man

   who ate it!

Ms. Moore: Yes, that's right, Yuko. When did it happen?

Yuko: I forgot if _____ .
   (3)

Dan: I know that! It happened in the 18th century. I wonder whether or not

   _____ .
   (4)

Mike: He did! He really liked it and thought it was a great idea! But I can't remember if

   _____ .
   (5)

Yuko: Yes, it is the name of a place, but for some reason I can't remember whether

   _____ .
   (6)

Dan: It's in England. I wonder if _____ .
   (7)

Mike: I don't know, but it's very popular nowadays, right?

2 Read the headline from an article about a new refrigerator. Then rewrite the sentences by replacing *whether* with *if.* When *if* is not possible, write ✗. Change the positions of *or not* when necessary.

> # Scientists Work on Low-energy Refrigerator Based on 1930 Einstein Patent
> ### Full article on page 6

1. I don't know whether or not Einstein's refrigerator worked.

   I don't know if Einstein's refrigerator worked or not.

2. Einstein probably thought about whether he'd make money from his creation.

   ✗

3. He certainly cared about whether the refrigerator would be good for the environment or not.

   _____

4. Some people couldn't figure out whether or not Einstein's invention was practical.

   _____

5. I'd like to find out whether today's version is practical.

   _____

6. The researchers had to decide whether to share the information with the public.

   _____

7. I don't know whether or not today's version will have financial success.

   _____

3 Rewrite the sentences about the invention contest finalists. Use the words in parentheses and *or.*

1. **Rafael:** I don't know which one will win.

   I don't know if the Ring Phone or the

   Scooter Shoes will win.

   (if)

2. **Betsy:** I don't care which one will make more money.

   _____

   _____

   (whether)

3. **Ted:** They're trying to decide which one will get first prize.

_____

(if)

4. **Mia:** I don't remember which one my cousin invented.

_____

(whether)

5. **Lori:** I'm trying to find out which one will get a patent first.

_____

(if)

6. **Ahmet:** I can't figure out which one will be more practical.

_____

(whether)

Noun Clauses in Direct and Indirect Questions

1 Rewrite the questions about an invention: "hair" that comes in a can. Use the words in parentheses and the correct punctuation.

1. What are the world's worst inventions? (Do you know)

   Do you know what the world's worst

   inventions are?

2. Who invented hair that comes in a can? (I was wondering)

   _____

   _____

3. How does the product work? (Can you explain)

   _____

4. Why would someone want to put colored powder on his or her head? (I'd like to know)

   _____

5. Does anyone buy this product? (I want to find out / if)

   _____

6. Does the product really look like hair? (Can anyone tell me / whether)

   _____

2 Rewrite each question as a direct or indirect question. Sometimes more than one answer is possible.

1. Do men or women use hair that comes in a can? (direct question)

   Do you know whether men or women use hair that comes in a can? OR

   Can anyone tell me if men or women use hair that comes in a can?

2. Can you use it on animals? (indirect question)

   _____

3. What colors does it come in? (direct question)

   _____

4. How much does it cost? (indirect question)

   _____

5. Can you buy it in stores or online? (direct question)

   _____

Avoid Common Mistakes

1 Circle the mistakes.

1. I don't know **if Tom's umbrella is for the rain or snow**. He has tested different
   (a)
   materials, but he's having trouble deciding **either he'll make it with plastic or nylon**.
   (b)
   Do you have any idea **whether or not you'd use it**?
   (c)

2. I don't know **what my friend is inventing**. I doubt **if his invention will be successful**.
   (a)   (b)
   I wonder **when will he finish**.
   (c)

3. The company wants to know **if anyone would buy their product**. They also want to
   (a)
   find out **wether it would be more popular with teenagers or adults**. They need to
   (b)
   know **whether or not it's easy to use**.
   (c)

4. John has to decide **either or not to return his cell phone**. I sometimes really wonder
   (a)
   if the company knows what a terrible product the phone is. But that's not
   (b)
   important. What is important is **whether they will give John his money back or not**.
   (c)

5. Do you know **wether or not Julie fixed her invention**? I heard from some friends
   (a)
   that it doesn't work well in bad weather. Do you know **if it works when the weather is good**?
   (b)   (c)

6. Can you help me with my invention? I need to figure out **either or not it's a good idea**.
(a)

   Please tell me **whether you like it or not**. It is very important to me to know **what you think**.
   (b)   (c)

7. I can't remember **whether my grandparents have a computer**. I think
   (a)

   that they have one, but I don't know **wether they think it's a good invention or not**.
   (b)   (c)

8. I was wondering **how this works**. Actually, I can't really figure out **what is it**, and I don't
   (a)   (b)

   know **who invented it**.
   (c)

2 Find and correct the mistakes in the information sheet about the Inventor's Fair.

Inventor's Fair – Judge's Information

It's time again for the Inventor's Fair. Thank you for being a judge. Please keep these things in mind when you judge the projects.

- It doesn't matter what age ~~is~~ the inventor ^is^. Anyone can win.

- If you don't know what is the invention, read the description.

5 • Test the invention to see either it works or not.

   As you test each invention, ask yourself these questions to help you pick a winner.

- Can anyone figure out how the invention works?

- Can you tell wether or not the invention would be useful in daily life? Whom would it help?

10 • Do you know wether the invention is unique or not? Does it already exist?

- It shouldn't matter either or not you like it. Judge the invention on if it is a good idea or not. How useful is it to people?

- The inventors read your comments either they're good or bad. If you don't like the invention, please write your comments politely.

Self-Assessment

Circle the word or phrase that correctly completes each sentence.

1. I wonder _____ restaurant first sold a sandwich.

   a. whether   b. what   c. when

2. I can't remember _____ invented the digital camera.

   a. who   b. if   c. that

3. I don't know what _____ about the new product.

   a. says   b. is saying   c. to say

4. I decided _____ to market my invention.

   a. how   b. what   c. if

5. You shouldn't forget _____ why you invented that.

   a. that   b. if   c. about

6. Do you know where _____ the information?

   a. finds   b. to find   c. if find

7. They don't care _____ or not that invention works.

   a. why   b. whether   c. if

8. I can't figure out _____ this invention works.

   a. what   b. which   c. if

9. I don't know whether to buy an older phone _____ the newest model.

   a. or   b. if   c. and

10. I haven't _____ whether or not to get a patent for my invention.

    a. remembered   b. decided   c. mattered

11. We should forget about _____ people will buy this and just create what we want.

    a. whether   b. if   c. or

12. _____ who invented the televison?

    a. Can you tell me   b. I was wondering   c. I don't know

13. _____ how to make a camera.

    a. Can anyone tell me   b. Do you know   c. I need to find out

14. Are you trying to find out _____ ?

    a. where the inventor   b. where the inventor is   c. where is the inventor

15. Do you know _____ ?

    a. whether his invention   b. did his invention   c. if did his invention
       won first place   win first place   win first place

Direct Speech and Indirect Speech

Human Motivation

Direct Speech

1 Complete the article with *asked* or *said*.

It is important to be motivated at work, and people have done a lot of research that shows what motivates employees. We wanted to know, however, what makes people feel *unmotivated* at work. We interviewed several experts in the field, and we <u>asked</u>, "What makes people feel unmotivated about
(1)
their jobs?" Dr. Luiza Brito _____ , "Boredom[1]
(2)

makes people very unmotivated." Dr. Nicholas Peters agreed. He _____ , "People
(3)
are not motivated to do their jobs well when they become bored with the things they are supposed to do." Eight of the ten experts we asked had a similar opinion. "When people don't feel challenged,[2] they are not motivated to do their best," _____ Andrea Ledger,
(4)
an author and motivational speaker.

"Whose fault is it when employees aren't motivated?" we _____ . "Is it the
(5)
employees' fault or is it management's[3] fault?" Dr. Brito _____ , "It's management's
(6)
fault. Employers need to find ways to motivate their employees." Dr. Peters had a slightly different opinion. "It's the responsibility of both the employees and the employers to make sure people are motivated," he _____ . Ms. Ledger had yet another opinion. She
(7)
_____ , "Why should managers motivate us?" When we expressed surprise at her
(8)
question, she _____ , "Not all work is fun and interesting. Employees need to find
(9)
ways to motivate themselves no matter what the work is."

---

[1]**boredom:** a state of being uninterested | [2]**challenged:** given an interesting or difficult task to do | [3]**management:** the people who run a company

2 Read the conversation. Then rewrite the sentences in bold as direct speech, showing who said or asked them. The information in parentheses shows you where to put the reporting clauses – at the beginning, in the middle, or at the end of the sentences.

Kyle: Hey, everyone. I read this interesting article about motivation. It made

me think about what motivates me. Now I have a question for you.

What motivates you to get out of bed in the morning?
<u>   (1)   </u>

Jing: **Breakfast motivates me to get up, and I always look forward to a cup of coffee.**
                                     (2)

Dana: **Nothing motivates me to get out of bed!**
                    (3)

Kyle: Very funny, Dana! Ian, **what about you?**
                                (4)

Ian: **The sunrise motivates me.** I like to take pictures of it.
                (5)

Kyle: **It's interesting that everyone's answer was different.**
                            (6)

Jing: Hey, Kyle, **what about you? What motivates you to get out of bed?**
                                   (7)

Kyle: **The Internet!** I like to read articles online when I get up in the morning.
         (8)

1. (beginning)

   Kyle asked, "What motivates you to get out of bed in the morning?"

2. (middle)

   _____

3. (beginning)

   _____

4. (end)

   _____

5. (end)

   _____

6. (beginning)

   _____

7. (beginning)

   _____

8. (end)

   _____

3 Unscramble the sentences about motivation. Use direct speech and add all the correct punctuation. Sometimes more than one answer is possible.

1. you / at work / what / motivates / Dan asked

   "What motivates you at work?" Dan asked. OR *Dan asked, "What motivates you at work?"*

2. Carol said / helps me / exercising during lunch / at work / stay motivated

   _____

3. motivated / keep me / at work / my deadlines / said Erica

   _____

4. a waiter / so I'm / said Josh / motivated / by tips / I'm

   _____

5. Rafael said / hard / motivates me / my manager / to work

   _____

6. don't need / I'm / external motivation / said Alison / because / I / naturally motivated

   _____

7. to get up / in the morning / said Chris / motivates me / my job

   _____

8. at your job / difficult / to find / Max asked / is it / motivation

   _____

Indirect Speech

1 Rewrite each quote as indirect speech. Use a reporting verb and change the main verb in each quote to express a past time.

Julie Mattes: "The class is very motivating."
Greg Thompson: "The students learned about the 19th century."
Debbie Morris: "History is an interesting subject."
Dan Ito: "The teacher is talking about inspiring leaders on Tuesday."
Laila Bhati: "The class is going to a history museum."

Review: History 101

We asked people about several classes at Thomson Community College.

Here's what students said about History 101. Julie Mattes, a history

major, _said that the class was very motivating_ . Greg Thompson

(1)

_____ . Debbie Morris, who

(2)

is an English major, _____ .

(3)

We asked students what topics the class covered. Dan Ito gave an example.

He _____ .

(4)

The students not only learn in the classroom, but they also often go on trips.

Laila Bhati _____ . Students clearly

(5)

enjoy this class at TCC.

2 Read the sentences about Dr. Andrews's advice to Marc O'Hallaran, a professional tennis player who has broken his arm. Then circle the word or phrase that completes each sentence with indirect speech.

1. Dr. Andrews said, "You have to do exercises so your arm can heal."

   He said that Marc _____ exercises so that his arm_____ .

   a. might do . . . can heal   (b. had to do . . . could heal)   c. had . . . might heal

2. Dr. Andrews said, "You shouldn't play tennis for at least eight weeks."

   He said that Marc _____ tennis for at least eight weeks.

   a. shouldn't play   b. might play   c. ought to

3. Dr. Andrews said, "You may be able to lift light weights after six weeks."

   He said that Marc _____ light weights after six weeks.

   a. can lift   b. might be able to lift   c. won't be able to lift

4. Dr. Andrews said, "You will need to work a long time to be 100 percent recovered."[1]

   He said that Marc _____ a long time to be 100 percent recovered.

   a. must need to work   b. would need to work   c. should work

---

[1]**recovered:** completely well, no longer injured

5. Dr. Andrews said, "You must work hard, and you have to stay motivated."

He said that Marc _____ hard, and that he _____ motivated.

a. might work ... could stay   b. could work ... could stay   c. had to work ... had to stay

6. Dr. Andrews said, "You ought to ask your trainer to help you focus."

He said that Marc _____ his trainer to help him focus.

a. asked   b. was going to ask   c. ought to ask

Indirect Speech Without Tense Shift

1 Read the advice people gave Brian about how to stay motivated at work. Then rewrite the bold sentences as indirect speech. Use *said* in the reporting clause and the same verb form as the direct speech in the reported sentence. Change the pronouns and use names when necessary.

Brian: I need help. **I'm having a problem staying motivated at work**. What should
(1)
I do?

Diego: **There are many ways to remain motivated during difficult times at work**.
(2)
Be creative!

Joe: I agree with Diego. **I avoid distraction by not checking my e-mail all day**.
(3)

Tong: Joe has a good point. **Checking e-mail wastes a lot of time**.
(4)

Brian: Thanks, everyone, but **I don't check e-mail very often at work**. Any
(5)
other ideas?

Adam: I was having problems staying motivated on the project I'm working on now
because it seems so endless. Then **I broke my work down into small parts**.
(6)
It's really helping!

Erin: Make a calendar with your deadline on it so you have a goal to work toward.
Calendars really help me stay on schedule.
(7)

1. _Brian said that he's having a problem staying motivated at work._

2. _____

3. _____

4. _____

5. _____

6. _____

7. _____

2 Complete the sentences with indirect speech. Write sentences that are true for you.

1. When I talk to my friends or colleagues about motivation, they say _____

_____ .

2. My English teacher usually says _____

_____ .

3. A good friend of mine always says _____

_____ .

4. People usually say _____ , and I agree with that.

_____ .

5. When people talk about motivation, they say _____

_____ , but I don't think that's always true.

6. When people are unmotivated, sometimes they say _____

_____ .

Other Reporting Verbs

1 Complete the sentences about a class assignment. Circle the correct reporting verbs.

1. Mr. Watson (informed) / explained the class that they had to give speeches.

2. Chuck **confessed / notified** to Mia that he was nervous about giving his speech.

3. Mia **mentioned / told** Chuck that she was also nervous.

4. Mia's older sister **reminded / explained** to them that they didn't need to get nervous.

5. She **swore / informed** that Mr. Watson had always given good grades when she was in his class.

6. She **convinced / replied** Mia and Chuck that they should relax before the speech.

2 Complete the sentences about exercising. Rewrite the second sentence as indirect speech. Use names as the object after the reporting verbs, and add *to* when necessary. Sometimes more than one answer is possible.

1. **Dan:** What's the best way to lose weight?
   Kiran: Every doctor has a different opinion!

   Kiran complained _to Dan that every doctor had a different opinion_ .

2. **Beatriz:** When I work out, I like to motivate myself by keeping track of my progress.
   Paul: Listening to music is also a good way to stay motivated.

   Paul mentioned _____ .

3. **Ji Ah:** I just got an e-mail from the gym. I wonder what it's about.
   E-mail: The gym will be closed on Sunday.

   An e-mail notified _____ .

4. **Cory:** I'm glad we both decided to exercise more. How is your exercise plan going?
   Pablo: It isn't going well at all.

   Pablo admitted _____ .

5. **Amanda:** This is hard. How can I stay motivated and keep running for another half hour?
   Charlie: The results will be worth it.

   Charlie assured _____ .

6. **Anne:** Did anyone meet the weight loss goal?
   Camila: Jill lost ten pounds last month.

   Camila reminded _____ .

7. **Claire:** What is a good class to take for fitness?
   Javier: Yoga will help with fitness.

   Javier explained _____ .

Avoid Common Mistakes

1 Circle the mistakes.

1. I **admitted to Donna** that I didn't know what "boredom" meant. Donna (**explained me**)
   (a)   (b)

   that "boredom" is what you feel when you're not interested in something or when there

   is nothing interesting to do. "Thank you for telling me," I **said**.
                                                                              (c)

2. Tom said, "**Martin Luther King, Jr. is** my greatest hero of all time." He also said that
                     (a)

   Nelson Mandela inspired him. He also said, **I met him on a plane five years ago**.
         (b)   (c)

3. Jocelyn said, **This motivational workshop is expensive**. She asked me,
                                    (a)

   "**Are you going to attend it**?" I told her that **I was going to**.
             (b)   (c)

4. Dustin said that **he has accomplished** a lot in life because he was self-motivated. He
                            (a)

   told me **he hadn't looked up to** any heroes at all. He said, "**I can't think** of anyone who
                  (b)   (c)

   inspired me."

5. Janice and Bob **complained** that their son wasn't motivated. They **admitted to me** that
                (a)   (b)

   he had no internal motivation. I **mentioned them** that they could motivate him with
                                              (c)

   rewards.

6. The motivational speaker said, "**Follow your dreams.**" She also said, **Goals are important**.
                                        (a)   (b)

   She explained that **making money should not be your only goal**.
                                     (c)

7. My grandfather **told me** to work hard. He **explained to me** that work is one of the most
                   (a)   (b)

   important things in life. He also **admitted me** that it was important to have fun once in
                                       (c)

   a while.

8. "**Music motivates me,**" Mariana said, **when I'm feeling bored**. Then she asked me,
         (a)   (b)

   "**Do you listen to music for motivation?**"
                      (c)

2 Find and correct the mistakes in the article about using music for motivation.

Music for Motivation

    Music can be very motivational. Dr. Olivia Halston said, ⌄" Music can make difficult jobs seem easier."⌄ She explained us that music affects the brain. She said that she have discovered that music makes the brain happy. We wanted to know how music motivates our readers, so we did an online survey to ask about their music habits over a one-month

5 period. Many readers said that they listen to music for motivation when they exercised during that time. For example, Lien, a 22-year-old nurse, said, I listen to music on my headphones when I exercise. She reported us that it made her workout go faster. Other readers admitted us that they listened to music when they did housework. Jack, a student, said that next Saturday he will probably play music by the Rolling Stones when he

10 cleaned the house. "It won't make cleaning fun," he said, but it will make it better.

Self-Assessment

Circle the word or phrase that correctly completes each sentence.

1. Jenna _____ "Nelson Mandela inspires me."

   a. "said"   b. said   c. said,

2. Hanan said, "I listen to music when I _____

   a. run.   b. run".   c. run."

3. "I am not challenged at work," _____ "so I'm bored."

   a. said Eric,   b. said Eric   c. said Eric,"

4. "What music do you listen to when you clean the house?" Jane _____ .

   a. told   b. asked   c. admitted

5. Phil asked, _____ time is the motivational speaker coming?"

   a. What"   b. "What   c. what

6. Matt said, "I don't work well early in the morning."

   Matt said that he _____ well early in the morning.

   a. doesn't work   b. won't work   c. isn't working

7. The manager said, "Alex worked the hardest last week."

   The manager said that Alex _____ the hardest last week.

   a. will work   b. had worked   c. works

8. Maria said, "You can sign up for the talk on motivation online."

   Maria said that I _____ sign up for the talk on motivation online.

   a. could   b. might   c. had to

9. Liz said, "Augusta is the capital of Maine."

   Liz said that Augusta _____ the capital of Maine.

   a. is   b. had been   c. is being

10. Barbara said, "Most people in my office are not motivated anymore."

    Barbara said that most people in her office _____ motivated anymore.

    a. hadn't been   b. haven't been   c. weren't

11. I _____ that the race would be difficult.

    a. told to you   b. told you   c. told

12. Jill _____ that it was too hot outside to be motivated to do anything.

    a. remarked   b. reminded   c. informed

13. Larry _____ me that I should join a gym. He thinks I'll be more motivated to exercise regularly.

    a. complained   b. remarked   c. convinced

14. Zai _____ to us that the office would close so that all the employees could attend the talk on motivation.

    a. notified   b. assured   c. reported

15. The survey _____ that 80 percent of the people were not motivated by money.

    a. confessed   b. reported   c. replied

Indirect Questions; Indirect Imperatives, Requests, and Advice

Creative Problem Solving

Indirect Questions

1 Read the conversation about product sales. Then label the indirect questions *T* (true) or *F* (false). Rewrite each false sentence to make it true.

Ms. Ortega: Our sales are very low this year. Does anyone have any ideas for ways to increase sales?

Bin: How low are our sales?

Ms. Ortega: They're 25 percent below last year's sales. We
5 need to think of creative methods to improve them.

Marta: Can we start selling our products online? I think that would increase sales.

Ms. Ortega: That's a good idea.

Bin: I agree. When would we be able to start selling items online? Do you think it
10 would take a long time to start online sales?

Ms. Ortega: I think it would take at least six months. What can we do to improve sales until then?

Marta: We can advertise online even before people can buy products online. Does the company have a page on a social media website?

15 **Ms. Ortega:** No, we don't, but that's a good idea. Who could create a page for us?

Bin: Do you remember Ed Jones? He used to work here in the IT department,[1] and now he works from home. We could hire him to help us.

Ms. Ortega: That's a great idea. Do you have Ed's contact information?

Bin: Yes, I do. I'll e-mail it to you after the meeting.

---

[1] **IT department:** Information Technology department; the group of workers at a company responsible for the company's computers

1. Ms. Ortega asked her employees if they knew why sales were low.

   F   Ms. Ortega asked her employees if they had any ideas for ways
   to increase sales.

2. Bin asked how low their sales were.

   _____ _____

3. Marta asked if they could stop selling their products online.

   _____ _____

4. Bin asked where they would be able to start selling items online.

   _____ _____

5. Bin asked if Ms. Ortega thought it would take a long time to start online sales.

   _____ _____

6. Marta asked if the company had a page on a social media website.

   _____ _____

7. Ms. Ortega asked who could sell a page for them.

   _____ _____

8. Bin asked Ms. Ortega if she remembered Ed Jones.

   _____ _____

9. Ms. Ortega asked Bin if he knew Ed.

   _____ _____

2 Unscramble the indirect questions.

1. he / if / had time / Fen asked / to talk / Jack

   Fen asked Jack if he had time to talk.

2. unhappy / she / Fen / Jack asked / if / was / at work

   _____

3. until 6:00 p.m. / she / if / him / Fen asked / had to / work

   _____

4. she / a problem / Fen / if / Jack asked / had / with her work schedule

   _____

5. Jack / Fen asked / she / if / to pick up her children / could / leave early

_____

6. with her babysitter / she / Fen / had a problem / Jack asked / if

_____

7. would / work from home tomorrow / if / Fen asked / Jack / be allowed to / she

_____

3 Rewrite the questions as indirect questions. Make any necessary changes to pronouns.

1. Jill asked Dan, "Are you still having problems with your computer?"

   Jill asked Dan if he was still having problems with his computer .

2. Dan said, "Yes, I am." Then he asked Jill, "What can I do about it?"

   Dan said he was and _asked Jill what he could do about it_ .

3. Jill asked Dan, "Have you reported the problem yet?"

   _____ .

4. Dan asked Jill, "Where can I report the problem?"

   _____ .

5. Jill asked, "Have you talked to the IT department?"

   _____ .

6. Then Jill asked, "Do you want me to go with you?"

   _____ .

7. Dan said, "No. That's OK." Then he asked Jill, "Who is the manager of the department?"

   Dan said that it was OK. Then _____ .

8. Jill asked, "Do you know Andre?"

   _____ .

9. Dan said, "I do." Then he asked, "Do you want to get some lunch?"

   Dan said he did and then _____ .

Indirect Imperatives, Requests, and Advice

1 Read the article about people's advice for thinking creatively. Then rewrite the statements in bold. Use infinitives and the reporting verb *said*.

≫ How to Think Creatively ≪

What are the best ways to think creatively? We asked people in different fields what their opinions were. This is what they said.

♦ "You never know when a good idea will come to you. **Carry a notebook and a pen at all times.** Then you can write down good ideas when you get them."

5   – *John Merchant, author*

♦ "**Listen to music.** It's a great way to open your mind." – *Mercedes Rivera, singer*

♦ "**Brainstorm ideas.** That's what I do when I need a creative solution to a problem." – *Bob Hu, web designer*

♦ "I know one thing not to do. **Don't watch TV.** TV kills creativity!" – *Naresh Gupta,*

10   *photographer*

♦ "**Read as much as possible.** Books exercise your brain and help you think about things in different ways." – *Anne Lawrence, teacher*

♦ "**Don't sit at a desk all day.** If you can't think of a solution to a problem, go for a walk. When you come back, you'll see things differently." – *Rich Simpson, manager*

15 ♦ "I have a trick that really helps me. **Meditate for 20 minutes every day.** Meditation is relaxing and helps you be more creative in problem solving." – *Teresa McDonald, editor*

♦ "**Exercise at least four times every week.** Exercise helps you focus on what's really important and gets rid of stress." – *Sophie Aitchison, accountant*

20 ♦ "**Talk to friends and colleagues.** Sometimes they have ideas that can really work." – *Paul Medeiros*

---

1. John Merchant <u>*said to carry a notebook and a pen at all times*</u> .

2. Mercedes Rivera _____ .

3. Bob Hu _____ .

4. Naresh Gupta _____ .

5. Anne Lawrence _____ .

6. Rich Simpson _____ .

7. Teresa McDonald _____ .

8. Sophie Aitchison _____ .

9. Paul Medeiros _____ .

2 Read these sentences about the advice Dr. Taylor, an expert problem-solver, gives to people. Then rewrite Dr. Taylor's statements. Use *told* or *asked* with infinitives.

1. Claire told Dr. Taylor that she was upset with her employees. Dr. Taylor said, "You should try to be patient."

   Dr. Taylor told her to try to be patient.

2. Mike explained to Dr. Taylor that he was very stressed at work and couldn't sleep at night. Dr. Taylor said, "Don't drink soda or coffee after 11:00 a.m."

   _____

3. Josh and Eileen told Dr. Taylor that they weren't communicating about their problems very well. Dr. Taylor said, "You should write down your problems before discussing them."

   _____

4. Martin sent text messages to his friend while he was talking about his problem. Dr. Taylor asked, "Would you please stop using your phone?"

   _____

5. We told Dr. Taylor we couldn't agree on where to go for vacation. Dr. Taylor said, "Don't worry about small problems."

   _____

6. Chris asked Dr. Taylor if they could meet on Wednesday. Dr. Taylor asked him, "Could we meet on Thursday instead?"

   _____

7. Janet and Bob tried to ignore their problems instead of talking about them. Dr. Taylor said, "Don't ignore problems when they occur."

   _____

8. Stephanie explained to Dr. Taylor that she didn't like her job, but didn't know how to find another one. Dr. Taylor asked, "Have you looked online for job opportunities?"

   _____

9. Nayoung asked Dr. Taylor if he could send his bills to her insurance company. Dr. Taylor asked, "Could you talk to my receptionist about your bills?"

   _____

10. Larry and Denise didn't arrive on time for their appointments. Dr. Taylor told them, "You need to learn to manage your time better."

    _____

Avoid Common Mistakes

1 Circle the mistakes.

1. Our boss (**asked us that we talk**) about our problems. She **told us to work** together
   (a)   (b)
   to find alternative solutions to traditional problems, and she **told us to listen** to each
                                                                      (c)
   other's ideas with an open mind.

2. Sharon asked me **if I liked** to solve problems. She asked me **how I solved** them
                    (a)   (b)
   creatively, and then she asked me **did I ever have** a problem I couldn't solve.
                                       (c)

3. Mauricio **said to be** on time for the meeting. He **told us to bring** pen and paper, and he
             (a)   (b)
   told we'd be brainstorming.
    (c)

4. Mrs. Harris **asked did I want** to lead the meeting. She asked **if I had been** in charge
                (a)   (b)
   before. She was hoping I'd say yes, but she asked **who would do** it if I couldn't.
                                                       (c)

5. My friend Tom **told me to stop** complaining, and my brother **told my problems** were
                  (a)   (b)
   small. Then Julie **asked why I was** so upset.
                       (c)

6. Mr. Moore told the students **to do** their homework, and he said that **there were** 10
                                (a)   (b)
   math problems. He asked **them that they solve** them creatively.
                            (c)

7. John asked Carol **why she was** late to the meeting. He asked her **did she have** a
                     (a)   (b)
   problem. She said she did have a problem, and he asked her **if he could** help.
                                                               (c)

8. The speaker **told to sit** down at the beginning of his presentation. During the
                (a)
   presentation, he **asked a man** to be quiet. Finally, when he was finished speaking, he
                     (b)
   asked us if we had any questions.
    (c)

2 Find and correct the mistakes in the article about jobs for creative people.

Top Jobs for Creative People

Are you a creative person? Dr. Lydia Garcia, a counselor who helps people find jobs,

to go
says ~~that we go~~ after the job of your dreams. Here are some great jobs for creative people.

Interior Designer: We asked interior designer Julie Newton did she think her job was

creative. She told that it was. She explained that interior designers need to be creative

5 with colors, patterns, and light.

Photographer: Photographers need to have a creative eye. We asked photographer

Cory Davis could he tell us the most important tip for being a good photographer. He said

that we be unique and not to do what everyone else does.

Teacher: Teachers have to think of creative ways to help students learn. Teacher

10 Debbie Morgan has 25 students. She says that she's always thinking of new ways to help

her students learn. She tells to do their best, and she helps them do it.

Chef: Good chefs are creative chefs. People like a variety of different kinds of foods. We

asked Chef Asami Tanaka did she think it was important to be creative in the kitchen. She

told that it was. She explained that people want food that tastes good, but they also want

15 it to look nice.

Are any of these jobs for you? Whatever you do, follow Dr. Garcia's advice. She said

that you find a job that's right for you.

Self-Assessment

Circle the word or phrase that correctly completes each sentence.

1. Rob asked if we _____ the meeting on time.

   a. would starting   b. would start   c. to start

2. Catalina asked Hank if he _____ a problem at work.

   a. will have   b. could have   c. had

3. **A:** What did the IT tech just tell you? **B:** She asked if her colleague _____ my problem.

   a. fixes   b. to fix   c. had fixed

4. The president asked if I _____ a new manager yet.

   a. to hire   b. were hiring   c. had hired

5. My boss asked us _____ to read the company's report.

   a. not to forget   b. to not forget   c. forget

6. Juan asked Melanie _____ she had a pen.

   a. who   b. did   c. if

7. He asked us _____ write down our problems.

   a. if we to   b. if we would   c. if would we

8. My boss asked, "Who helped you solve the computer problem?"

   My boss asked me who _____ solve the computer problem.

   a. helped her   b. had helped us   c. has helped you

9. Valeria asked Lei _____ to discuss the problem.

   a. when wanted she   b. when she wanted   c. when did she want

10. Kelly asked _____ I wanted to be a photographer.

   a. to me if   b. that   c. me if

11. Our teacher asked us _____ together on the project.

   a. to work   b. we work   c. she worked

12. Tatiana said _____ her when she has a problem.

   a. not to help   b. to help not   c. not help

13. Erol asked _____ the meeting early.

   a. leave   b. to leave   c. he could leave

14. She _____ to everyone's ideas.

   a. asked to listen us   b. asked listen   c. asked us to listen

15. He _____ Ivan to help him.

   a. asked me   b. asked   c. said

The Passive (1)

English as a Global Language

Active vs. Passive Sentences

1 Read the sentences about a new English word used by some Spanish speakers. Label the sentences A (active) or P (passive).

1. __P__ English is spoken around the world.

2. _____ Sometimes nonnative speakers create new "English" words.

3. _____ The word *coolisimo* is being used by some English speakers whose first language is Spanish.

4. _____ *Coolisimo* means "very cool."

5. _____ The Spanish ending -*isimo* was added to the English word *cool*.

6. _____ The word *coolisimo* is spread by people who speak both Spanish and English.

7. _____ Most native speakers of English probably have not heard the word *coolisimo*.

8. _____ Is the word *coolisimo* understood by most native English speakers?

2 Rewrite the sentences about the use of English around the world. Use the passive. Do not use an agent.

1. People in many places speak English for many reasons.

   English is spoken in many places for many reasons.

2. People use English at airports and train stations.

   _____

   _____

3. People type commands in English on computers.

   _____

4. People are writing e-mails in English.

   _____

5. People make announcements in English at international events.

   _____

✈	Izlazi **Gates**	→
🛄	Carinska kontrola **Customs control**	→
🛂	Pasoška kontrola **Passport control**	→

6. People hear English songs in many places.

_____

7. How do people use English in your country?

_____

8. Are people conducting business meetings in English?

_____

9. Do the schools ask students to read English-language books?

_____

3 Complete the article about Cyber-English. Use the present perfect form of the passive with the verb in parentheses.

Since the late twentieth century, a special term _has been used_ (use) by some people
(1)

on the Internet. The term _____ (call) Cyber-English. Cyber-English
(2)

is the use of English when talking about things related to computers and technology.

Often, words found in computer directions _____ (not translate)
(3)

into different languages. Instead, words _____ (take) directly from
(4)

English for use in the directions. English words such as *click*, *e-mail*, and *link* often remain

in these directions. As a result, these words _____ (learn)
(5)

by people around the world, perhaps without them even realizing it. The world

_____ (bring) closer together by the use of computers, and
(6)

Cyber-English is an example of this.

4 Complete the article about English in India. Circle the correct forms of the passive.

Today, English (is spoken) / was spoken in many parts of India, but that wasn't always
(1)

true. In the early 1800s, English **is not being used / was not being used** widely there. The
(2)

use of English became more common after India became part of the British Empire

in 1858. After that, in the late 1800s, English universities **are started / were started**. Since
(3)

then, English **has been spread / was spread** by the education system. Today, in addition
(4)

to the local languages, English **is also being taught / was also being taught** in most
(5)

schools.

At the state level, a number of languages **have been made / are made** official in India,
(6)
including Hindi, Bengali, Urdu, and Punjabi, but English has become a very important

language for communication in the country. Nowadays, English **is used / was used** for
(7)
private and business communication between speakers of different languages in India.

Business meetings **are being conducted / were being conducted** in English. And even
(8)
some government documents **are being written / were being written** in English.
(9)

5 Read the article on the Manx language. Cross out the *by* + agent phrases in bold if the
information is not important or if the meaning of the sentence is clear without it.

For many years, Manx was spoken ~~**by people**~~
(1)
on the Isle of Man. In 1765, the Isle of Man was sold

by the Duke of Atholl. It was sold **by the Duke**
(2)   (3)
to the British. After that, English was used

by more and more people on the island. The Manx
(4)
language began to disappear. In 1961, it was spoken

by fewer than 200 inhabitants. People on the island
(5)
were concerned about the loss of their language. The

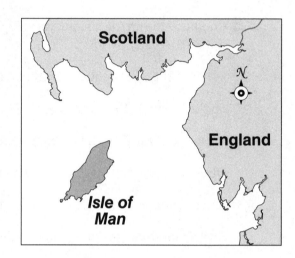

language was regarded **by the people** as an important part of their culture. In 1985, a
(6)
resolution was passed **by the government** to give Manx official recognition. More people
(7)
began speaking Manx, and it was taught **by teachers** in schools. By 2001, Manx was being
(8)
used **by over 1,500 people**, and today it is considered **by people** an important language
(9)   (10)
again.

Verbs and Objects with the Passive

1 Read the sentences about the Latin alphabet. Label the sentences *T* (transitive) or
I (intransitive). Then rewrite the transitive sentences in the passive. Sometimes more than
one answer is possible.

1. __*T*__ English writers use the Latin alphabet.

   The Latin alphabet is used by English writers.

2. _____ The Latin alphabet appears in written English, French, and many other languages.

3. ____ Many people around the world use the Latin alphabet.

_____

4. ____ The Latin alphabet started over 2,000 years ago.

_____

5. ____ The Romans created a writing system based on earlier alphabets.

_____

6. ____ Many letters in the Latin alphabet also appear in the ancient Greek alphabet.

_____

7. ____ In fact, the word *alphabet* comes from the first two letters of the Greek alphabet.

_____

8. ____ Eventually, there were 23 letters in the ancient Roman alphabet.

_____

9. ____ Many tourists to Italy easily recognize letters on ancient Roman monuments.

_____

2 Read the sentences about a movie on the English language. Label the words in bold *DO* (direct object) or *IO* (indirect object). Then rewrite the sentences in the passive. Make the words in bold the subjects of the sentences. Sometimes more than one answer is possible.

1. _DO_ The teacher showed the class **a movie** about the history of English.

   A movie about the history of English was shown to the class by the teacher.

2. _____ The narrator told **the audience** the history of English since the fifth century.

   _____

3. _____ The narrator offered the audience **examples of changes in the language over the centuries**.

   _____

4. _____ The moviemakers showed **viewers** some of the varieties of spoken English.

   _____

5. _____ English speakers from different places gave **the moviemakers** samples of speech.

   _____

6. _____ The narrator showed **the differences between British English and American English**.

   _____

Reasons for Using the Passive

1 Complete the steps for a language study. Use the simple past form of the passive with the verbs in parentheses.

Step 1: A survey _was developed_ (develop) by language experts in Canada.
$\qquad\qquad$ (1)

Step 2: One hundred people _____ (include) in the survey about
$\qquad\qquad\qquad\qquad\qquad$ (2)

language. They were all from the province of Quebec.

Step 3: The participants _____ (ask) about what languages they
$\qquad\qquad\qquad\qquad\qquad$ (3)

spoke at home. About 80 percent answered French.

Step 4: The answers _____ (examine) by an expert. The expert
$\qquad\qquad\qquad\qquad\qquad$ (4)

found interesting results.

Step 5: The results _____ (compare) to results from a similar
$\qquad\qquad\qquad\qquad\qquad$ (5)

survey in New Brunswick. In New Brunswick, approximately 30 percent of people

speak French at home.

Step 6: The results and conclusions _____ (publish) in a report.
$\qquad\qquad\qquad\qquad\qquad\qquad\qquad$ (6)

2 Look at a reporter's notes for a podcast. Then complete the podcast with the passive form of the verbs in the notes.

Sign language

1) A person is teaching sign language to chimpanzees at Lovitt Zoo.

2) The person has presented 20 words to the chimpanzees.

Language survey

3) An organization in our city conducted a survey last year.

4) Experts published the results last week.

5) People speak foreign languages more frequently than ever before.

Most popular foreign language

6) I made a mistake in my previous podcast.

7) I reported the most popular foreign language at Lovitt High School incorrectly.

8) More high school students are studying Chinese, not Japanese.

Hello. It's Tim Gradey with *Language News*. This is an interesting story.

Sign language _is being taught_ to chimpanzees at Lovitt Zoo. Twenty words
               (1)

_____ so far, and the trainer thinks the chimpanzees
           (2)

are capable of learning many more.

    Next, some fascinating results are in from a recent survey. A language survey

_____ in our city last year, and the results
           (3)

_____ last week. The results show that foreign languages
           (4)

_____ more frequently in our city than ever before, and
           (5)

the trend is sure to continue.

    Finally, a mistake _____ in my previous
           (6)

podcast. The information about the most popular foreign language at Lovitt High

School _____ incorrectly. Chinese, not Japanese,
           (7)

_____ by more high school students.
           (8)

    That's all for now. Tune in next time . . .

Avoid Common Mistakes

1 Circle the mistakes.

1. Portuguese **is spoken** in several countries around the world. It **is used** by more than
          (a)   (b)
175 million native Portuguese speakers. My cousins **have been studied** Portuguese for
                                    (c)
five years.

2. What countries **is Portuguese spoken** in now? In the past, what countries
                 (a)
was it spoken in? Why **it was made** the official language of Brazil?
    (b)   (c)

3. English **is using** by approximately 330 million native speakers, and some people
        (a)
estimate it **is used** by another 500 million nonnative speakers. It **is spoken** by
          (b)   (c)
approximately 830 million people in total.

4. Chinese **is spoken** as a first language by over one billion people. Spanish **spoken** as a
        (a)   (b)
first language by over 300 million people. As a first language, Arabic **is used** by over 200
                                             (c)
million people.

5. The local languages **weren't used** at the business meeting. The meetings **conducted** in
   (a)   (b)
   English. The speakers **were understood** by everyone.
   (c)
6. That book **was written** in Japanese. It **is being translating** into several languages. It
   (a)   (b)
   is also being made into a movie.
   (c)
7. Where **the movie was filmed?** **Was it made** in India? What awards
   (a)   (b)
   were the moviemakers given?
   (c)
8. The movie **was made** in Canada. The actors **were spoken** French, so the producers
   (a)   (b)
   have included English subtitles.
   (c)

2 Find and correct the mistakes in the paragraph about English use around the world.

English Your Way

        used
English is ~~use~~ in many countries around the world. It is sometimes a difficult language

to learn. Pronunciation known to be difficult for some people. For example, the *j* as it is

pronouncing in English words (like *June*) can be difficult for Spanish speakers. That is

because the same sound does not occur in Spanish. Vowels are also difficult for most

5 learners of English. Many vowel sounds are finding in English. Americans are used about

fifteen vowel sounds. Also, the vowel sounds pronounced a bit differently in different

places in the English-speaking world. Learners have been found ways to improve their

pronunciation in English for a long time. Many pronunciation classes are offering at

schools. People also listen to native speakers to improve. What pronunciation tips you

10 were taught? Which ones are you using?

Self-Assessment

Circle the word or phrase that correctly completes each sentence.

1. A survey about a global language _____ on a website.

   a. is be conducted   b. is being conduct   c. is being conducted

2. The word *smog* _____ by combining *smoke* and *fog*.

   a. was formed   b. form   c. be formed

3. Esperanto _____ today, but not by many people.

    a. is spoken   b. was being spoken   c. be spoken

4. The use of words in both Spanish and English _____ *Spanglish*.

    a. is calling   b. called   c. is called

5. People _____ to vote for the best choice for a global language.

    a. are being asked   b. is being asked   c. was being asked

6. Esperanto _____ in 1887.

    a. was developed   b. was develop   c. is being developed

7. A utensil that is like both a spoon and a fork _____ .

    a. is a *spork* called   b. is called a *spork*   c. a *spork* is called

8. New languages _____ without success.

    a. have often be   b. have often been   c. has often been
       developed   developed   developed

9. The website says that languages such as English, Spanish, and Esperanto _____ for
   the best global language.

    a. are considering   b. are being considered   c. considered

10. Many languages _____ at the international assembly.

    a. were being speaking   b. was being spoken   c. were being spoken

11. Esperanto _____ at a language conference I attended last year.

    a. were being spoken   b. is being spoken   c. was being spoken

12. Eurolang _____ in the 1990s as a language for the European Union.

    a. was creating   b. was create   c. was created

13. Eurolang was developed _____ .

    a. by   b. by Philip Hunt   c. Philip Hunt

14. Esperanto _____ to be an easy language.

    a. designed   b. was designing   c. was designed

15. The Pirahã language _____ many people.

    a. has never been spoken by   b. has never been spoken   c. has never be spoken by

The Passive (2)

Food Safety

The Passive with *Be Going To* and Modals

1 Complete the interview about genetically modified (GM) foods. Write questions with the words given. Then complete the two answers. Use the passive with *will*. An agent is not always necessary.

1. world hunger problems / solve / by GM foods

   Interviewer: *Will world hunger problems be solved by GM foods*?

   Dr. Rivera: Yes, they *'ll be solved by GM foods*. Countries can grow more of these crops.

   Dr. Simms: No, they *won't be solved by GM foods*. Better food distribution is the solution.

2. public concerns about GM food safety / reduce

   Interviewer: _____?

   Dr. Rivera: Yes, they _____.
   Up to now, there have been no incidences of illnesses from GM foods.

   Dr. Simms: No, they _____.
   The safety of GM foods has not been proven.

3. more and more GM foods / purchase / by consumers

   Interviewer: _____?

   Dr. Rivera: Yes, more GM foods _____.
   The foods are being sold in more places.

   Dr. Simms: No, more GM foods _____.
   People are going to buy more organic foods.

4. the safety of GM foods / confirm / by research

   Interviewer: _____?

   Dr. Rivera: Yes, it _____.
   Experts will be doing more studies.

   Dr. Simms: No, it _____.
   Studies will continue to show mixed results.

5. GM foods / regulate / more strictly / by more countries

Interviewer: _____ ?

Dr. Rivera: No, they _____ .
Many countries, like Great Britain, already have good regulations.

Dr. Simms: Yes, they _____ .
More countries are looking into the dangers of GM foods.

2 Complete the introduction to a book about genetically modified food. Use the passive form of the verbs in parentheses with *be going to* or the present perfect. Sometimes more than one answer is possible.

GM Food: Beware

Introduction

The pros and cons of genetically modified (GM) food *have been discussed* (discuss) a lot over
(1)
the years, and the topic _____ certainly _____ (talk) about even more in the
(2)   (2)
future. The purpose of this book is to provide consumers with reliable information on what is already

known about GM food and its potential risks.

A lot of research _____ (do) over the past years on GM food, and
(3)
the results are usually not positive. For example, mice _____ (use)
(4)
in experiments on GM rice since 2008 in one laboratory. The experiments show the mice's

immune systems were damaged by eating the rice. These results tell us that it is possible people

_____ (harm) by GM rice in the future. This is only one example. Several
(5)
examples _____ (give) in this book that show other dangers of GM food.
(6)
More GM food research _____ (do) in the future, and it will likely
(7)
show more harmful effects of GM food. Some GM crops _____ (grow)
(8)
since the 1990s. They _____ (not test) properly or thoroughly, however,
(9)
they _____ (make) available for consumers. We still do not know all of
(10)
the effects of these products, but we know that in the future, it is quite possible that the negative

effects _____ (see) in people.
(11)
This book might not be read by the people who have the power to stop growing GM food, but I

hope that it will at least encourage the reader to stop consuming GM food.

3 Complete the sentences about the pros and cons of GM foods. Use the passive form of the verbs in the boxes with the modals in parentheses.

Pros

~~grow~~	keep	modify	sell

1. GM crops _can be grown_ (can) without harmful pesticides.

2. GM foods _____ (may) to be much richer in nutrients[1] than they are now.

3. GM foods _____ (might) at lower prices if supermarkets pass cost savings on to consumers.

4. Some GM foods _____ (could) fresh longer if they were designed that way.

Cons

cause	damage	know	test

5. Harmful effects of GM foods on humans _____ (may not) yet.

6. Local environments _____ (could) by GM crops.

7. GM foods _____ (must) more thoroughly.

8. Health problems in humans _____ (might) by GM foods.

---
[1]**nutrient:** a substance that is required by living things to live and grow

4 Read the announcement from a conference on GM food. Then write opinions about the statements. Write sentences that are true for you. Use the passive with *should* (*not*).

> Good morning, and welcome to the Conference on GM Food. I'm going to start by telling you a few things that are going on in the field today.
>
> 1) Tests are being done on animals to find out the effects of GM food on humans.
>
> 2) GM crops are being sold before they are tested for long periods.
>
> 3) GM rice is being given to people in poor areas.
>
> 4) Identification labels are being put on GM products in supermarkets.
>
> 5) Brochures about the issues related to GM foods are being made available in supermarkets.

1. _____

2. _____

3. _____

4. _____

5. _____

Get Passives

1 Complete the podcast about food recalls. Use *get* passives in the simple present with the verbs in parentheses.

      Welcome to the "Food Safety" podcast. Today, we're talking about food recalls. Food _gets recalled_ (recall) when it is dangerous to people. This means that stores can no
(1)

longer sell the product because there's something wrong with it. One major reason food is

recalled is because it _____ (contaminate) by a substance that will harm
              (2)

people. Salmonella is one type of bacteria that makes food dangerous. It can be found on

meat that _____ (not cook) thoroughly enough. It's also found
              (3)

on fruits and vegetables that _____ (not wash) properly. Another
                      (4)

reason food is recalled is because an object _____ (drop) into the food. For
                        (5)

example, plastic or paper could accidentally _____ (put) into a food item at
                    (6)

a factory. Most organizations take food safety seriously and recall items when they might

potentially harm the public. Be sure to tune in next week's podcast about safe food storage.

2 Look at the chart about food being recalled. Then write sentences with *get* passives in the present progressive (for the food) and in the simple past (for the reason).

	Product	Recalled	Reason
1.	chicken	Yes	contaminated with salmonella
2.	frozen potatoes	Yes	labeled incorrectly
3.	fish	No	not contaminated
4.	chocolate milk	Yes	not processed correctly
5.	hot dogs	No	not damaged by bacteria
6.	fruit drinks	Yes	not packaged correctly

1. _The chicken is getting recalled because it got contaminated with salmonella._

2. _____

3. _____

4. _____

5. _____

6. _____

3 Read the interview with the owner of ChedCheese. Find seven more passive verbs and change them into *get* passives.

Interviewer: Last week, 1,000 cases of cheese made by ChedCheese, Inc. ~~were~~ *got* recalled. Today, the owner of ChedCheese, Mr. John Harris, is here to talk with us about the problem. Hello, Mr. Harris, and thank you for coming.

Mr. Harris: You're welcome. Thank you for having me.

5 **Interviewer:** So, tell us about the problem.

Mr. Harris: Well, several people became sick after eating our cheese, so all of our cheese products were tested by the FDA.

Interviewer: I see. And what did the FDA find?

Mr. Harris: They found that one of our cheeses had been contaminated.

10 **Interviewer:** So, what happened?

Mr. Harris: That cheese was recalled by the FDA. Of course, at ChedCheese, we are concerned about public safety. I personally made an announcement about the recall.

Interviewer: Do you know how the cheese was contaminated?

15 **Mr. Harris:** Yes, I do. Unfortunately, several of my employees did not follow our safety procedures.

Interviewer: And what happened to those employees? Were they fired?

Mr. Harris: Yes, I fired them. At ChedCheese, we take safety seriously.

Interviewer: Your company was shut down, right?

20 **Mr. Harris:** Yes, but it wasn't shut down by the government. I decided to close the factory and do a thorough cleaning of our equipment. We're going to reopen on Monday, and I want consumers to know it will be safe to buy our cheese again.

Interviewer: Thank you for your time, Mr. Harris.

Passive Gerunds and Infinitives

1 Complete the conversation with the correct passive form of the verbs in parentheses.

Rob: Hi, Sofia. Look at this article about unhealthy foods. Aren't you tired of

being told (tell) what to eat all the time?
(1)

Sofia: Not really. I like _____ (inform) about what is good and
(2)

bad for me. For example, I learned that canned food can be really unhealthy.

One reason is that it has a lot of salt.

Rob: Yes, but when I read some of these food safety articles, I manage

_____ (persuade) that all food is bad!
(3)

Sofia: Well, I guess you can't be afraid of _____ (harm) by all food,
(4)

but you should avoid canned food.

Rob: I don't agree. Over the past few years, a lot of canned foods seem

_____ (improve) by food companies. They have a lot less
(5)

salt and more nutrients. And sometimes it's just easier to heat something up than to

make it!

Sofia: Maybe, but some people complain about _____ (misinform).
(6)

Sometimes companies make canned foods seem healthy when they're really not.

Rob: Well, I don't expect _____ (mislead) by every food label I read.
(7)

Aren't there laws about giving false information on a food label? Besides, I don't think

it matters what you eat as long as you exercise. And eating canned food gives me more

time to go to the gym!

Sofia: Rob! Exercise isn't enough if you have an unhealthy diet!

2 Complete the information from a brochure on food safety at home. Use *being* or *to be*.

1. People usually want _to be_ informed about food safety problems at home.

2. People who wash their hands regularly are less likely _____ infected by
   germs in their kitchens.

3. People are usually interested in _____ shown how to prepare food safely.

4. Some people seemed _____ surprised to hear that the most commonly
   contaminated food at home is meat.

5. Most people are concerned about _____ harmed by contaminated food in their homes.

6. Some people don't expect _____ harmed by the food that they buy.

3 Complete the statements about food safety. Circle the correct words. Then check (✓) *Agree* or *Disagree* to show your opinion.

	Agree	**Disagree**
1. **I expect /** **I'm worried about** being harmed by bad food.	☐	☐
2. **I enjoy / I want** to be informed about food safety.	☐	☐
3. **I hope / I avoid** to be told about food recalls.	☐	☐
4. **I refuse / I'm afraid of** being exposed to germs in my kitchen.	☐	☐
5. **I'm interested in / I seem** being educated about the food I eat.	☐	☐
6. **I'm not likely / I'm afraid of** to be persuaded to buy unhealthy food.	☐	☐

Avoid Common Mistakes

1 Circle the mistakes.

1. Many genetically modified (GM) animals **will probably be created** in the future. These
   (a)
   animals **will be use** to produce medicine. Many people **will be concerned** by this
   (b)   (c)
   development.

2. Animals **can be created** to produce material for drugs that fight diseases in humans.
   (a)
   Some people think that these animals **should make** to help people. Others think that
   (b)
   people **could be harmed** by GM animals.
   (c)

3. The FDA **has put** restrictions on creating GM animals. A guide to how GM animals
   (a)
   are controlled **has been publish**. Some consumers **have been confused** about the
   (b)   (c)
   guidelines.

4. GM animals **might use** for food, too. All food from GM animals **is going to be checked**
   (a)   (b)
   by the FDA before it **can be sold**.
   (c)

5. Medicine made from GM animals **must be approved** by the FDA. The first medicine
   (a)
   was made from the milk from a GM goat. Patients **should tell** when their medicine is
   (b)   (c)
   created from a GM animal.

6. Some people think that medicines that were developed using GM animals

   should not be approved by the FDA. They think that these drugs **should be test** before
   (a)   (b)

   they are approved and their possible dangers **should be studied** for a longer period.
                                                         (c)

7. All medicines **should be tested** thoroughly before they are sold. Problems
                               (a)

   can be found with new medicines. Numerous tests **must perform** before new
   (b)   (c)

   medicines are sold.

8. Rules **should make** about labeling GM products before they go on the market. For
                     (a)

   example, GM foods in supermarkets **could be labeled** with special stickers. Consumers
                                                     (b)

   should be informed about all possible dangers from the very beginning.
                       (c)

2 Find and correct eight more mistakes in the paragraph about a local farmers' market.

Community to Approve Farmers' Market

approved
A farmers' market will formally be ~~approve~~ by the community board at its next

meeting. Farmers' products will be sell at a market downtown every weekend. The market

will be inspect by the health board before it opens in May. The health board needs to give

final approval. A wide variety of freshly grown products will be display for consumers

to choose, including fruits, vegetables, and flowers. In addition, products such as honey

might be include on the list of items available. GM foods won't sell at the market,

however. Cooking demonstrations may schedule for some weekends. More information

can find on the city's website. This market will be enjoy by families throughout the

community.

Self-Assessment

Circle the word or phrase that correctly completes each sentence.

1. More food hybrids, crosses between two foods, _____ in the near future.

   a. will be developed   b. will be develop   c. will developing

2. GM foods should be _____ in supermarkets.

   a. label   b. labeled   c. labeling

3. Did the professor's paper on the benefits of GM foods _____ published?

   a. be   b. get   c. is

4. Broccoli and cauliflower can _____ crossed to produce "broccoflower."

   a. been   b. be   c. being

5. Organic foods are not likely _____ found at that supermarket.

   a. to be   b. be   c. being

6. More medicine from GM meats is _____ be created in the future.

   a. to go to   b. going   c. going to

7. Some people think food hybrids might be _____ more in the future.

   a. eat   b. eats   c. eaten

8. The article on pesticides _____ in the newspaper tomorrow.

   a. will not be published   b. not will be published   c. will not published

9. I'm concerned about _____ exposed to chemicals in my food.

   a. being   b. to be   c. be

10. Do you think these food labels could _____ ?

    a. understood   b. be understood   c. everyone be
       by everyone   by everyone   understood by

11. The scientists _____ to be given approval by the FDA.

    a. succeeded in   b. expected   c. missed

12. The proposal to develop GM fish _____ last week.

    a. got approved   b. got approve   c. approved

13. _____ GM animals be raised on your farm?

   a. Do   b. Will   c. Are

14. The animals on our farm _____ food with pesticides. We are aware of the potential risks.

   a. aren't feeding   b. are not going to feed   c. are not going to be fed

15. _____ people be harmed by GM animals created for medicine? This is a good question for your debate.

   a. Do   b. Are   c. Could

Subject Relative Clauses (Adjective Clauses with Subject Relative Pronouns)

Alternative Energy Sources

Identifying Subject Relative Clauses

1 Read the paragraph about a family's use of geothermal energy. Underline the relative clauses and circle the nouns they refer to.

Helen and David Mitchell are (people) who live in Michigan. Michigan

is a U.S. state that has very cold winters. In the winter, the Mitchells had

heating bills which were over $600 a month. They did a lot of research to

see how they could save money on their heating bill. Geotime is a company

that installs a type of geothermal energy system. It is a system which is put

underground. It uses heat from the ground to heat the home. Mr. Reynolds

is a man who works for Geotime. He came to the Mitchells' house to explain

the system, and they decided to have it installed. It has been very successful.

In January, the Mitchells had a heating bill that was only $115!

2 Complete the conversation about alternative energy sources in a community. Use the words in parentheses with the simple present.

Luisa: Are you interested in finding out about the types of alternative energy

which are (which / be) available in our community? I belong to a group
(1)

_____ (that / help) the public learn more about green energy.
(2)

David: Sure. What options are available for people _____ (who / live) here?
(3)

Luisa: Well, there's wind energy. It's energy _____ (which / be) from
(4)

windmills. The power company _____ (that / run) the windmills
(5)

charges a little extra for the energy from them. There's also solar power. There are

many local companies _____ (that / install) solar panels.
(6)

David: Isn't the equipment _____ (which / collect) energy from the sun expensive?
(7)

Luisa: It can be. But solar energy pays off over time. Geothermal energy is a type of energy

_____ (which / save) people a lot of money.
(8)

3 Rewrite the sentences about an environmental organization. Replace *that* with *which* or *who*.

1. The Clean Power Campaign is an organization that started over 20 years ago.

   The Clean Power Campaign is an organization which started over

   20 years ago.

2. Clean Power Campaign was started by people that wanted to make a difference.

   _____

3. Clean Power Campaign employees talk to companies that use a lot of dirty fuels.

   _____

4. Employees that work for Clean Power Campaign encourage those companies to use renewable energy.

   _____

5. The organization contacts government agencies that make decisions about energy use.

   _____

6. Clean Power Campaign speaks to the agencies on behalf of citizens that are concerned about clean energy.

   _____

4 Read part of a glossary of green energy terms. Then complete the sentences with relative clauses.

> **green:** a word describing something good for the environment
>
> **greens:** people supporting environmental organizations or political parties
>
> **green business:** a business selling products or services that do not harm the environment
>
> 5 **green-collar worker:** a person working for a green business or an environmental organization
>
> **green energy:** energy not harming the environment when produced or consumed
>
> **greenhouse gases:** gases trapping the sun's heat and causing a rise in
>
> 10   temperature

1. *Green* is a word _that describes something good for the environment_ .

2. *Greens* are people _____ .

3. A *green business* is a business _____ .

4. A *green-collar worker* is someone _____ .

5. *Green energy* is energy _____ .

6. *Greenhouse gases* are gases _____ .

Nonidentifying Subject Relative Clauses

1 Combine the sentences about green roofs. Make the second sentence a nonidentifying relative clause.

1. Green roofs help the environment. Green roofs are gardens on the tops of buildings.

   Green roofs, which are gardens on the tops of

   buildings, help the environment.

2. Energy costs can be reduced by green roofs. Green roofs keep heat out in the summer and keep heat in during the winter.

   _____

3. People put gardens on the tops of buildings. Gardens can include trees and flowers.

   _____

4. Trees and large plants are grown in one type of roof garden. This type of garden is also called an intensive roof garden.

   _____

5. Intensive gardens can seem like parks in the sky. The intensive gardens need a thick layer of soil.

   _____

6. Another kind of roof garden has low-growing plants in thin soil. This kind of garden is called an extensive roof garden.

   _____

7. My cousin grows carrots and peppers in his extensive garden. He is a professor researching green roofs.

   _____

2 Write sentences with identifying or nonidentifying clauses. Use the sentence in bold to help you.

1. **I have two sisters with different jobs.**

   My sister / is a conservationist / is visiting tomorrow

   My sister who is a conservationist is visiting tomorrow.

2. **The type of car is additional information.**

   Ivan's car / is a hybrid / gets good gas mileage

   _____

3. **We have one uncle.**

   Our uncle / is an electrical engineer / has an electric car

   _____

4. **There are two companies called NRG in different locations.**

   The NRG / is located on Main Street / sells only eco-friendly products

   _____

5. **The number of employees is additional information.**

   Geotime / has 30 employees / installs geothermal systems

   _____

6. **Paulina works in two offices.**

   Paulina's office / is downtown / uses solar energy

   _____

Subject Relative Clauses with *Whose*

1 Complete the opinion letter to a newspaper. Circle the correct verbs. Then underline the nouns that the verbs agree with.

Vote on Energy by Stephanie Price

We need to support leaders whose main goal (is)/ **are** to use renewable energy sources.
(1)
Alex Nelson, whose parents **owns / own** a green company, is running for mayor. He works as a
(2)
lawyer at Crawford & Hu. Pat Crawford, who started the law firm and whose practice **is / are**
(3)
well known, helps preserve green spaces. Nelson's experience makes him a great candidate.

Rita Levins, whose volunteer activities in the community **is / are** numerous, is also
(4)
running for mayor. Levins, whose father **has worked / have worked** in a coal mine, supports
(5)
using coal as an energy source. She has served on the town council. Levins may be a
qualified politician, but she does not support renewable energy.

Jennifer Chen, whose campaign promises **includes / include** support for renewable
(6)
energy, is the third candidate for mayor. Chen, whose parents **owns / own** a gardening
(7)
business, has experience with green issues. However, Chen's main issue is support for
education, whose funding[1] **has been cut / have been cut**.
(8)
In my opinion, you should vote for Alex Nelson, whose experience **makes / make** him
(9)
the best person for the job.

_____

[1]**funding:** money made available for a particular purpose

2 Underline the relative clauses with *whose* in the sentences about building an energy-efficient home. Then label the relative clauses *I* (identifying) or *NI* (nonidentifying). Add commas to the sentences with nonidentifying relative clauses.

1. _NI_ Yesterday I spoke with my mother, whose cousin is Maria Sanchez.

2. _____ The Sanchezes are the family whose dream is to have an energy-efficient house.

3. _____ The Sanchez family are friends with someone whose company designs energy-efficient homes.

4. _____ Gloria Ramirez whose company is a family business will design their home.

5. _____ Gloria whose children all work in the business has two daughters and a son.

6. _____ Gloria's daughter whose specialty is eco-friendly home design will design the interiors.

7. _____ Gloria's son whose specialty is geothermal energy will install the heating system.

8. _____ These relatives of mine whose home is being built this year are pleased with the plans.

3 A Match the information about people and companies that won green awards to their actions.

1. _d_ Johanna Berenson, author   a. Her design for a green roof won an award.

2. _____ Laura Akpem, architect   b. His decisions led to cleaner energy for the city.

3. _____ Marcos Avilez, actor   c. Its windows are very energy-efficient.

4. _____ Eco-Car, a car company   d̶. Her books are about green energy.

5. _____ James Peters, politician   e. Its hybrid cars are some of the cleanest vehicles sold in the United States.

6. _____ Good Green Home Group, a remodeling company   f. His latest movie is about a worldwide energy crisis.

B Write sentences with the information from A. Use identifying subject relative clauses with *whose*.

1. _Johanna Berenson is an author whose books are about green energy._

2. _____

3. _____

4. _____

5. _____

6. _____

4 Complete the review of a book about green homes. Use *who* or *whose*.

Johanna Berenson, <u>*whose*</u> newest book reached number one on the best-seller list
          (1)

yesterday, has written several books on green energy. In her newest book, she gives advice

on how to have an energy-efficient home. Her advice is for homeowners _____ want
                                                                              (2)

to reduce the amount of energy they use. Her book is also useful for people _____
                                                                              (3)

want to build new homes that are green. Her book includes examples of people _____
                                                                              (4)

homes are already green. It is full of information and tips that will help anyone _____
                                                                              (5)

wants to go green get started. Whether you are someone _____ is new to green
                                                            (6)

building or someone _____ home is already green, you are sure to find useful
                        (7)

information in *Going Green: Home Edition*.

Avoid Common Mistakes

1 Circle the mistakes.

1. My parents, (which) believe in clean energy, have solar panels on their roof. Their house,
                 (a)

    which is on a hill, gets a lot of sunlight. Their heating bill, **which** is sent monthly, is
     (b)   (c)

    never very expensive.

2. I have a friend **who** is an electrical engineer. She works at a green energy company **that**
                    (a)   (b)

    is in Denver. She has a job **who** is very difficult.
                                  (c)

3. Tina works at the farmers' **market, which is** only open on Saturdays. She passes out
                               (a)

    fliers that they are about wind power. Her company hopes **people who take the fliers**
     (b)   (c)

    will switch to wind power.

4. The person **who's** house is for sale is Mr. Lee. His sons, **who** don't live at home anymore,
               (a)   (b)

    want to keep the house. The house, **which** has a green roof, is energy-efficient.
                                         (c)

5. In the future, we may have cars **which** run on biofuel. Imagine driving a car **who** runs
                                    (a)   (b)

    on oil from vegetables. Many plants **that** are rich in oil could be used for fuel.
                                          (c)

6. Matt is an **architect who he works** for a green company. His boss is a
               (a)

    woman who cares about the environment. The company's **houses, which are**
     (b)   (c)

    eco-friendly, are expensive to build.

7. Claudia Rodriguez is a politician **who** is running for mayor. She is a person **that** has
   (a)   (b)
   been a lawyer in the past. She is someone **which** is concerned about dirty fuels.
                                          (c)

8. Kyle Morgan, **whose** father is an inventor, is trying to convert his house into an
                 (a)
   eco-friendly home. For example, he is trying to make a swimming pool **that** doesn't use
                                                                        (b)
   chemicals. His father, **who's** inventions have won awards, is helping him design it.
                           (c)

2 Find and correct eight more mistakes in the article about making homes green.

> ### Go Green
>
> which OR that
> There are many things you can do to have a home ~~who~~ helps the environment. Install
>
> a solar panel system, which it heats your home with energy from the sun. You could
>
> also get a geothermal system, who heats your home with energy from the ground. A
>
> geothermal system, which it can be expensive at first, saves money over time. This type
>
> 5 of system, who heats your home cheaply, can also cool your home. You can find many
>
> people online which sell solar panels and geothermal systems. You could also put a green
>
> roof on your home. The roof, who helps to heat the home, can also be used for a garden.
>
> Green roofs, which need to be flat, work best on new homes. Find an architect who's
>
> company specializes in green roofs to build your home. There are many options for having
>
> 10 a home that it doesn't pollute the environment and saves you money on heating bills.

Self-Assessment

Circle the word or phrase that correctly completes each sentence.

1. Wind turbines _____ are in fields near our town generate power for a lot of the state.

   a. whose   b. who   c. that

2. People _____ live in my town are not happy because they do not get much wind power.

   a. whose   b. which   c. who

3. Farmers who _____ windmills on their land want more wind power on their farms.

   a. has   b. have   c. to have

4. My friends Keith and Kristy have a home _____ uses solar power.

   a. whose   b. which   c. who

5. Some houses that rely on the sun's energy have large windows that _____ as solar panels.

   a. work   b. they work   c. works

6. _____ design green roofs have interesting jobs.

   a. People   b. People, who   c. People who

7. _____ installs solar panels, is opening his own business.

   a. Jerry Richards, who   b. Jerry Richards who   c. Jerry Richards, which

8. Maria Torrez, _____ is an urban planner, designed the green roof on our building.

   a. who   b. that   c. which

9. The roof of City Hall, which _____ plants and flowers on it, won a Green Award.

   a. have   b. has   c. it has

10. Mei Parks, _____ is running for mayor, supports renewable energy.

    a. which   b. whose   c. who

11. My friends, whose home _____ geothermal energy, have very low heating bills.

    a. use   b. is   c. uses

12. We're going to a concert _____ profits will be donated to a renewable energy fund.

    a. whose   b. which   c. that

13. My _____ has a green home. My other sister wastes a lot of energy.

    a. sister, who lives   b. sister who lives   c. sister whose lives
       in Portland,   in Portland   in Portland

14. Did you read the article _____ was about dirty fuels?

    a. who   b. whose   c. that

15. Our car, _____ great gas mileage, runs partly on electricity.

    a. that get   b. which get   c. which gets

22 Object Relative Clauses (Adjective Clauses with Object Relative Pronouns)

Biometrics

Identifying Object Relative Clauses

1 Read the description of a TV crime show. Then underline seven more identifying object relative clauses and circle the nouns they refer to.

Forensic Files is a popular TV show. It shows (crimes) that experts solve with forensic science. Each episode is about a different crime which someone has committed. In many episodes, investigators use DNA that criminals have left at
5 the crime scene to help them solve the case. Because each person's DNA is unique, the DNA that the investigators collect is often important evidence. Once investigators find a suspect, they can match the suspect's DNA to the DNA that they have found at the scene. The DNA can show if a suspect was present at a crime scene. However, DNA is not the only forensic
10 evidence that these investigators use to solve the crimes. They also use fingerprints, footprints, and even clothing fibers that they find at the scene. Investigators on the show usually use forensics to catch criminals, but not always. Some of the suspects who they investigate are innocent. Forensic evidence, like DNA, can help show that, too.

2 Read the paragraphs about cold cases. Then cross out the relative pronouns that can be omitted.

Forensics can be used to solve cases ~~that~~ police consider "cold." Cold cases are investigations **that** police have not been able to solve – sometimes for over 20 years.

New technology **that** investigators didn't have in the past is available today, so crimes **which** people committed many years ago can eventually be solved. In one case, police
5 collected evidence from a crime **that** someone committed 30 years ago. The police found some hair at the crime scene, but the investigators couldn't prove **whose** hair it was. Thirty years later, the DNA in the hair **which** the police had found was tested. The hair matched one of the suspect's DNA, and he was arrested for the crime **that** he had committed years before.

Cold case investigators have an important job. People **whose** family members criminals
10 have hurt may feel satisfied when a person is arrested even after many years.

3 Combine the sentences in the descriptions of TV shows. Use identifying object relative clauses with *which* or *who*.

TV show	Description	
1. *Forensic Files*	Investigators use forensic evidence to solve crimes. Police find the forensic evidence at the crime scene.	
2. *Most Shocking*	Terrible crimes are shown. People around the world have committed these crimes.	
3. *Body of Evidence*	Dayle Hinman is an investigator. Viewers see her solve crimes with forensics.	
4. *CSI*	Forensic investigators analyze data. The police find the data at the crime scene.	
5. *Solved: Extreme Forensics*	Two unusual crimes are shown each week. Investigators solve the crimes with forensics.	
6. *Body of Proof*	A medical examiner studies victims for evidence. She uses the evidence to solve crimes.	

1. In *Forensic Files*, _investigators use forensic evidence which police find at the crime scene to solve crimes_ .

2. In *Most Shocking*, _____ _____ .

3. In *Body of Evidence*, _____ _____ .

4. In *CSI*, _____ _____ .

5. In *Solved: Extreme Forensics*, _____ _____ .

6. In *Body of Proof*, _____ _____ .

Nonidentifying Object Relative Clauses

1 Rewrite the sentences about Robert A. Leonard and forensic linguistics. Make the sentences in parentheses nonidentifying object relative clauses that add information about the words in bold.

1. Robert A. Leonard was in **the band Sha Na Na**. (People loved it in the 1970s.)

    Robert A. Leonard was in the band Sha Na Na, which people loved

    in the 1970s.

2. Leonard became interested in **linguistics**. (He now teaches it at a university.)

    _____

3. He enjoys teaching **forensic linguistics**. (He describes it as the newest tool in investigations.)

    _____

4. Leonard thinks that **language** is like a fingerprint. (Each person uses it in a unique way.)

    _____

5. **Leonard** can often identify people by how they write. (Police sometimes ask him for help.)

    _____

6. **Leonard** has helped the police solve many crimes. (*Forensic Files* once interviewed him.)

    _____

2 Combine each pair of lines of the conversation into one sentence. Make Nick's sentences into nonidentifying object relative clauses.

1. **Claire:** Sherlock Holmes is one of the most famous fictional detectives.

    Nick: Sir Arthur Conan Doyle created that character in the 1800s.

    Sherlock Holmes, whom Sir Arthur Conan Doyle created in the 1800s, is

    one of the most famous fictional detectives.

2. **Claire:** The first Sherlock Holmes mystery was *A Study in Scarlet.*

    Nick: People liked it immediately.

    _____

3. **Claire:** Holmes's most famous detective cases involved forensic evidence.

    Nick: He solved them with the use of logic.

    _____

4. **Claire:** Dr. Watson was Holmes's friend and assistant.

   Nick: Doyle uses Dr. Watson as the narrator for most of the stories.

   _____

5. **Claire:** In 2009, Robert Downey, Jr. played the detective in the movie _Sherlock Holmes_.

   Nick: Millions of people around the world saw it.

   _____

Object Relative Clauses as Objects of Prepositions

1 A Complete the interview with an author of a mystery book. Use the correct relative pronouns. Sometimes more than one answer is possible.

Interviewer: Now for our _Book It_ interview. Today we will speak to author Janice Jameson from Miami. She has written the best-selling book _Stranger Than True_, _which_ ✓ (1) I told you about before the break. So, tell us a little bit about your book, Janice.

Janice: Well, it's a fictional story about a murder that a detective named Martin is trying to solve. He arrives at a house _____ someone broke (2) into and finds very few clues.

Interviewer: Can you give us an idea how he solves the crime?

Janice: I can't tell you who the criminal is, but I can tell you Detective Martin finds a dog hair, _____ other investigators did not pay attention to. (3) This one dog hair is tested by forensic experts and helps him solve the crime.

Interviewer: Interesting . . . Your book, _____ you must have done research (4) on, is very realistic. Where did you find your information?

Janice: I have a cousin _____ I spoke with. He works in a forensic lab (5) in Miami. He gave me a lot of information about a case _____ (6) he worked on.

Interviewer: So, is there a real person _____ the main character is based on? (7)

Janice: Yes. Detective Martin is actually based on my husband!

Interviewer: Really? Is he a detective?

Janice: No, he's a teacher! Detective Martin's personality, _____

(8)

reviewers usually comment on, is like my husband's.

Interviewer: Well, it's a great book that I'm sure our audience will enjoy. Detective Martin

is an interesting character, and the forensics used to solve the crime are

fascinating. Thank you, Janice.

B Look at the conversation in A again. Place an ✗ above the relative pronouns that can be omitted. Place a check (✓) above the relative pronouns that are necessary.

2 Read the movie description. Then rewrite it with the prepositions before the relative pronouns when possible.

Conviction

The movie *Conviction*, which Hilary Swank stars in, was released in 2010. Betty Anne Waters is the real-life woman who the movie is based on. Betty Anne fights to prove her brother is innocent of a murder that he was convicted of. She enters law school, which she graduates from after years of study. She is determined to prove her brother is innocent of the crime that others say he is guilty of.

The movie Conviction, in which Hilary Swank stars, was released in 2010.

_____

_____

_____

_____

_____

Avoid Common Mistakes

1 Circle the mistakes.

1. A forensic tool **in which linguistics is used** is author identification. Experts,
(a)
(who police hire them), analyze threatening letters and e-mails. They compare the
(b)
threatening messages to other messages **that people have written**.
(c)

2. Voice identification, **who** investigators use to solve crimes, is a forensic technique.
(a)
Threatening messages **that** criminals leave on phones are analyzed. Investigators, **who**
(b)   (c)
victims contact, compare the messages to suspects' voices.

3. Wildlife **forensics, which** many people are just learning about, is a new field. It uses
(a)
animal DNA, which wildlife forensic scientists analyze. Many **crimes, that** criminals
(b)   (c)
commit against animals can be solved with its use.

4. **John, whose** father I work with at the police station, is studying forensics. He's taking
(a)
classes in forensic methods, **which** his father also studied. His father is a **person, whom**
(b)   (c)
John admires.

5. Donald Allison, **which** police caught at an airport, stole two rhinoceros horns. He was
(a)
getting on a plane with a fake antique piece **in which** the two horns were hidden. He
(b)
was arrested for the crime, **which** he had to spend one year in prison for.
(c)

6. *CSI: New York*, **which** Gary Sinise stars in, is a TV show about forensic investigators. The
(a)
show, **what** many people enjoy watching, is about crimes and the investigators who
(b)
solve them. Sinise plays Detective Mac Taylor, **whom** the other investigators respect.
(c)

7. TV shows **in which investigators use forensic evidence to solve crimes** have become
(a)
very popular. Criminals **who police arrest for crimes without forensic evidence**
(b)
are often not found guilty in trials. People on juries now expect forensic evidence,

which police cannot always find it at a crime scene.
(c)

8. Julia, **whose** taste in TV shows I admire, enjoys watching real-life stories. TruTV, **which**
(a)   (b)
she watches every night, is a station with shows about crimes. The shows **what** Julia
(c)
likes watching the most are about forensics.

2 Find and correct the mistakes in the article about the history of forensics.

The History of Forensics

Forensic science, ~~who~~ *which* many investigators use to solve crimes today, is not a new

science. Fortunatus Fidelis, which people call the founder of forensic medicine,

already practiced this type of medicine in the 1590s. Forensic medicine, what uses

medical evidence to solve crimes, has changed over the years. Here are some historic

5 developments:

1. Fingerprints, which criminals leave them at crime scenes, became a way to identify

    people in the late 1800s. However, computer systems what police use to scan, store,

    and compare fingerprints weren't created until the last half of the twentieth century.

2. In 1901, Karl Landsteiner discovered that people have different blood types. After

10   that, investigators could use blood samples that they found them at crime scenes to

    eliminate suspects.

3. In the 1980s, Ray White identified important features of DNA, who investigators now

    collect from almost every modern-day crime scene. In 1987, DNA was first used to

    prove that a man, who police thought had committed a crime, was guilty.

15   Technology in forensic science is always being developed, and there will be even more

    ways, that police can catch criminals in the future.

Self-Assessment

Circle the word or phrase that correctly completes each sentence.

1. Detectives are people _____ I admire.

   a. whose   b. who   c. which

2. Crimes _____ police couldn't solve in the past can sometimes be solved by using DNA.

   a. whose   b. who   c. that

3. My aunt, _____ I really respect, works in a forensics lab.

   a. whom   b. which   c. what

4. The investigators who the company _____ couldn't find any clues.

   a. hired them   b. hired   c. hired to

5. The victims _____ house the criminal broke into live on my street.

   a. which   b. whose   c. who

6. _____ people have studied for years, is now a degree program at some universities.

   a. Forensic science, which   b. Forensic science that   c. Forensic science, what

7. My favorite crime _____ many people watch, is *CSI*.

   a. show, which   b. show, who   c. show, that

8. That is the window that the criminal left his fingerprints _____ .

   a. them   b. whose   c. on

9. Detective Grendall, _____ Ted gave a statement, will handle the investigation.

   a. to who   b. to whom   c. to which

10. Police investigated the crime _____ was a witness.

    a. to which my brother   b. which my brother   c. to whom my brother

11. The apartment _____ was renting was robbed.

    a. what I   b. who I   c. I

12. The book *Crime Labs of the Future*, _____ I read for class, was about new forensic technology.

    a. whose   b. who   c. which

13. The witness, _____ , was late to the trial.

    a. who the defense   b. whom the defense   c. on which the
       relied   relied on   defense relied

14. Did you hear about the new book _____ the famous forensic anthropologist wrote?

    a. to whom   b. that   c. who

15. Investigators analyzed the letter _____ the murderer left at the crime scene.

    a. whose   b. what   c. which

Relative Clauses with *Where* and *When*; Reduced Relative Clauses

Millennials

Relative Clauses with *Where* and *When*

1 Complete the beginning of an article about Generation Z. Use *where* or *when*.

Generation Z

The United States is a country <u>where</u> people are often defined by their
(1)
generation. Generation Z is the youngest generation in the United States. Many

experts agree that the 2000s is the period _____ people in this generation were
(2)
born. This is a time _____ young people were exposed to a lot of technology. For
(3)
this reason, Generation Z is also called the *Internet Generation*. The Internet is the

place _____ many people in Generation Z "live." They communicate with each
(4)
other, play games, and do many other things on the Internet. They live in a world

_____ face-to-face communication isn't always necessary. Experts predict that
(5)
when people in Generation Z get older, it will be a time _____ many people will
(6)
work from home with computers.

2 Rewrite the sentences about Gen Xers, people born between 1965 and 1981. Use the simple present of *be*, relative clauses with *where*, and the words in parentheses.

1. Gen Xers tend to enjoy spending time in coffee shops. (places)

    Coffee shops <u>*are places where Gen Xers tend to enjoy spending time*</u>.

2. Gen Xers have introduced many new ideas on the Internet. (place)

    The Internet _____.

3. Many Gen Xers shop at Amazon.com. (website)

    Amazon.com _____.

4. Gen Xers like to go on adventure vacations in countries like Chile and Nepal. (locations)

    Countries like Chile and Nepal _____.

5. Gen Xers want to work at companies with opportunities for promotion. (places)

    Companies with opportunities for promotion _____.

3 Read the sentences about Internet use. Circle the relative clauses that are correct.

1. The 2010s are a time . . .   (in which many people use the Internet at home and at work.)

   which many people use the Internet at home and at work.

2. The Internet is a place . . .   where many young people communicate.

   that many young people communicate.

3. The 1990s were years . . .   when Internet use spread rapidly.

   during when Internet use spread rapidly.

4. South Korea is a country . . .   where most homes have Internet connections in.

   in which most homes have Internet connections.

5. This is the season . . .   in which most Internet applications start to sell.

   which most Internet applications start to sell.

Reduced Relative Clauses

1 Rewrite the sentences about generations. Use participle phrases and prepositional phrases. For adjectives, put the adjective before the noun.

1. Traditionalists are people who were born before 1946. They are people who are respectful.

   Traditionalists are people born before 1946. They are respectful people.

2. Baby Boomers are people who are optimistic. Most of them are people who are in their 50s and 60s.

   _____

   _____

3. Gen Xers are people who were born in the 1960s and 1970s. Gen Xers are people who are flexible.

   _____

   _____

4. Millennials are people who are looking for challenges. They are people who are educated.

   _____

   _____

2 Combine the sentences using appositives. Make the second sentence the appositive.

1. Tim Scott is a Gen Xer. He is a sociology professor at Clark Community College.

   Tim Scott, a sociology professor at Clark Community College, is a Gen Xer.

2. His son is a Gen Zer. He is a two-year-old.

   _____

3. Tim is doing research on China's Generation Y. China's Generation Y is the Chinese post-1980s generation.

   _____

4. Tim found out about Generation Y from Michael Stanat. Michael Stanat is the author of *China's Generation Y: Understanding the Future Leaders of the World's Next Superpower.*

   _____

5. According to Stanat, China's Generation Y is composed of approximately 200 million individuals. China's Generation Y is an entrepreneurial and tech-savvy group.

   _____

3 Look at the picture of a conference about Millennials. Then combine the sentences with sentences in the box. Use participle or prepositional phrases. Sometimes more than one answer is possible.

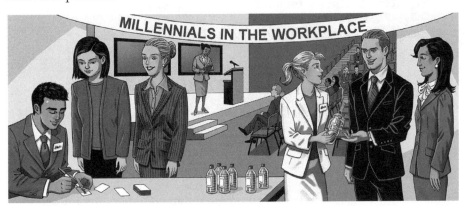

He is writing name tags.	She is speaking first at the conference.
It is on the information table.	~~The conference is titled "Millennials in the Workplace."~~
She is passing out the bottles of water.	The people are attending the conference.

1. The people are attending a conference.

   The people are attending a conference titled "Millennials in the Workplace."

2. The organizers think that most of the people are Millennials.

   _____

3. There is a man at the information table.

   _____

4. The water is for the attendees.

_____

5. There is a woman by the information table.

_____

6. The woman is already on the stage.

_____

Avoid Common Mistakes

1 Circle the mistakes.

1. The United States is a **country where people are** often defined by their generation. It
   (a)
   is a **place where changes are** always happening. It is a (**place where accept**) change
   (b)   (c)
   willingly.

2. The 1950s was the decade **when** the Beat movement started. It was a time **in when**
                            (a)   (b)
   writers criticized many things about society. It was a period **in which** poets wrote
                                                                   (c)
   personal and political poems.

3. My aunt, **a Baby Boomer**, has had the same job for 30 years. My cousin, **a Millennial**,
              (a)   (b)
   has had three jobs. My brother, **is a Gen Zer**, wants to work at home.
                                    (c)

4. Tech Serve is a café **where people can use the Internet**. It is also a place
                         (a)
   where can have great food. The chair **in which I like to sit** is near the window.
    (b)   (c)

5. 1920 to 1945 is the period **in when the Traditionalists were born**. 1946 to 1964
                               (a)
   is the period **that the Baby Boomers were born in**. 1965 to 1981 is the time
                  (b)
   when Gen Xers were born.
    (c)

6. John F. Kennedy, **was the president of the United States from 1961 to 1963**, was
                     (a)
   popular with Baby Boomers. Jack Kerouac, **who was a Beat Generation writer**, was
                                             (b)
   also popular with them. The Beatles, **a famous British band**, influenced many Baby
                                         (c)
   Boomers.

7. U2, **a band from Ireland**, is popular with Gen Xers. Bono, **is the lead singer for U2**,
   <u>(a)</u>   (b)

   writes most of the lyrics to their songs. The Edge, **who is the guitar player for U2**,
                                                               (c)

   writes a lot of the music.

8. 1929 is the year **when** the stock market crashed. 1963 is the year **in which** President
                             (a)   (b)

   Kennedy died. 1989 is the year **in when** the Berlin Wall fell.
                                  (c)

2 Find and correct seven more mistakes in the article about generation gaps.

Generation Gap

A generation gap is a difference in values and attitudes between two generations.

Sociologists, ~~are~~ people who study society, often examine generation gaps. The United

States is a country where have found gaps among generations.

The 1960s was a decade in when there was a big generation gap between

5 Traditionalists and Baby Boomers. Traditionalists, were the parents of the Baby Boomers,

were conservative. Their children, were the Baby Boomers, wanted to express their

personal freedom. It was a period in when the younger generation protested against

society and government. Big cities were places where often gathered to protest, sometimes

through music. Joan Baez, was a folk singer, sang protest songs. Many Traditionalists did

10 not like, or even understand, the music their children were listening to.

Self-Assessment

Circle the word or phrase that correctly completes each sentence.

1. The United States is a _____ where there is a lot of interest in defining generations.

   a. year   b. time   c. country

2. The Pew Research Center is a place _____ research is being done on generations.

   a. where   b. when   c. which

3. A 2008 Pew Internet & American Life Project survey showed that 30 percent of
   adults _____ the Internet were Millennials.

   a. using   b. who using   c. are using

4. Heather often does research on the computers _____ the library.

   a. where   b. in   c. which in

5. The Internet is a place _____ teenagers and young adults go to communicate with friends.

   a. in where   b. when   c. where

6. The 1930s was a time _____ many people were unemployed.

   a. when   b. in when   c. where

7. The 1930s was the period _____ the Traditionalists grew up.

   a. where   b. which   c. in which

8. The United States is a _____ many popular Internet sites began.

   a. country where   b. country when   c. country

9. Many members of Generation X, _____ *Gen Xers*, helped created the Internet as we know it.

   a. who called   b. called   c. were called

10. Japan is a country _____ very common.

    a. where the use of technology is   b. the use of technology is   c. where is

11. Kyle is one of the sociologists _____ generations for a government report.

    a. researching   b. who researching   c. is researching

12. Maria does all of the work _____ for the report.

    a. is required   b. that required   c. required

13. Gen Xers, _____ , make up 23 percent of people on the Internet, according to a 2008 Pew Internet & American Life Project survey.

    a. who now in their   b. now in their   c. are now in their
       30s and 40s   30s and 40s   30s and 40s

14. Joe's research shows Millennials are often _____ people.

    a. sociable   b. in which sociable   c. who are sociable

15. Millennials _____ with technology often socialize online.

    a. are familiar   b. who familiar   c. familiar

Real Conditionals: Present and Future

Media in the United States

Present Real Conditionals

1 Complete the sentences about becoming a photojournalist. Use present real conditionals with the simple present form of the verbs and the words in parentheses.

1. If _you do not want_ (you / not want) to work in an office every day,

   photojournalism is (photojournalism / be) a great career.

2. If _____ (you / be) a fair and ethical photojournalist,

   _____ (you / show) what you see and don't try to manipulate

   the image.

3. A _____ (photo / be) good when _____ (it / tell)

   a story without words.

4. _____ (you / need) to know how to use a variety of camera

   equipment if _____ (you / want) to be a photojournalist.

5. If _____ (someone / plan) to enter the field of photojournalism,

   _____ (there / be) many schools with strong programs.

6. When _____ (you / look for) a job or internship in the field,

   _____ (you / need) a portfolio of photos.

7. Often _____ (a person / not need) a photojournalism degree if

   _____ (he or she / have) a good portfolio.

8. Usually, _____ (people / try) to get assignments from news

   organizations if _____ (they / want) a job in the field.

9. If _____ (you / be) present at a major or interesting event,

   _____ (you / have) a chance to get a good photo to sell to a news

   organization or to add to your portfolio.

2 Write sentences about citizen journalism. Use present real conditionals with *if* and the information given. (The symbol → points to the main clause.) Write each conditional once with the *if* clause first and once with the main clause first. If a noun is repeated in the two clauses, use a pronoun in the second clause.

1. you are not a trained journalist and you report a story → it is called "citizen journalism"

   If you are not a trained journalist and you report a story, it is called

   "citizen journalism."

   It is called "citizen journalism" if you are not a trained journalist and you

   report a story.

2. an average person submits a news story → a news organization considers the story

   _____

   _____

3. the story is interesting → a news organization often uses the story

   _____

   _____

4. the news organization is good → the news organization checks the facts

   _____

   _____

5. the stories are not objective → a good news organization does not use the stories

   _____

   _____

3 Complete the conversation about news habits. Use present real conditionals with the words in parentheses and the simple present form of the verbs.

Valeria: How do you usually get the news?

Tracey: Well, I like to read the paper in the morning, but sometimes I get up too late.

Valeria: When *you don't read the paper* (you / not read / the paper),
                          (1)
_____ (what / you / do)?
                    (2)

Tracey: If I get up late, I usually listen to the news on the radio. I listen to it when I'm

   getting ready for work. There's a public radio station I really like.

Valeria: All right. And _____ (what / news sources / you / use)
                                       (3)
   if _____ (you / want / news on something specific)?
              (4)

Tracey: What do you mean?

Valeria: Well, you know, _____ (what / happen) if
_____(5)_____

_____ (you / want / to find out more about a story)?
_____(6)_____

Tracey: Oh, I usually look up news like that online. What about you?

_____ (what / be / your favorite news sources) when
_____(7)_____

_____ (you / want / to get more information)?
_____(8)_____

Valeria: I usually look up stories online, too. When _____
_____(9)_____

(my friends / post / interesting news stories) on social networking sites,

_____ (I / often / follow up) by finding similar articles
_____(10)_____

in news sources.

Tracey: When _____ (you / be / home after work),
_____(11)_____

_____ (you / watch / the news on TV)?
_____(12)_____

Valeria: Not very often. It's just so easy to get the news other ways.

Tracey: I agree!

4 Complete the sentences about news with information that is true for you. Emphasize the result by using *then*.

1. If I read the news online, _____ .

2. If there is a major story in the news, _____ .

3. If a story doesn't sound objective, _____ .

4. If my friends tell me about an important story, _____ .

5. If there are stories about natural disasters, _____ .

Future Real Conditionals

1 A Complete the conversation about bands. Use future real conditionals and the correct form of the verbs in parentheses.

John: The Ballyhoo Band is on the cover of *Music News*. They're playing at Brandow Center next

month. I really want to go. If I *have* (have) the money, I *'ll get* (get) a ticket this week.
_____(1)_____   _____(2)_____

Maria: You'd better buy it soon or they'll be sold out. If you _____ (wait) too
_____(3)_____

long, you _____ (not get) good seats.
_____(4)_____

John: Would you like to go with me?

Maria: I'd love to, but I can't. My cousin is getting married that weekend. If I

_____ (not go), my family _____ (be) really upset.
　　　　　(5)　　　　　　　　　　　　　　　　　　　(6)

John: Oh, is the wedding going to be here or in another city?

Maria: Well, it's going to be at the family country house, about an hour from here. The

wedding is going to be outside, so I hope the weather is good.

John: If it _____ (rain), what _____ they _____ (do)?
　　　　　　　　(7)　　　　　　　　　　　(8)　　　　　　(8)

Maria: They say that if the weather _____ (be) bad on the day of the
　　　　　　　　　　　　　　　　　　　　(9)

wedding, they _____ (put up) tents.
　　　　　　　　(10)

John: Well, I hope it doesn't rain – for their sake and for the concert's.

Maria: Me too. By the way, the Rock and Roll Hall of Fame induction ceremony is on TV

tonight. Are you planning to watch it?

John: Oh, I forgot about it entirely! I may have to work late tonight. Oh well, if I

_____ (miss) it, I _____ (watch) it online later.
　　　　　(11)　　　　　　　　　　　　　(12)

B Complete the sentences about the conversation in A. Use *even if* or *unless*.

1. _Unless_ John buys the tickets for The Ballyhoo Band concert soon, he won't be able to get good seats.

2. Maria won't be able to go to the concert _____ she wants to.

3. The wedding Maria is attending will be outside _____ the weather is bad.

4. _____ the weather is bad, they won't need tents for the wedding.

5. _____ John works late tonight, he will be able to watch the Hall of Fame ceremony online.

2 Answer the questions with future real conditionals and information that is true for you. If you write more than one result for the condition in your answer, don't repeat the *if* clause.

1. If you buy a magazine this week, what kind of magazine will you buy?

_____

2. If you get home early, will you watch the evening news? If not, what will you watch?

_____

3. What sites will you visit if you are online tonight?

_____

4. If you read an interesting article, will you try to find out more about the subject?

_____

Real Conditionals with Modals, Modal-like Expressions, and Imperatives

1 Complete the sentences about product reviews. Circle the correct modals.

1. If you want to buy a product online, you **(should)** / can't read reviews of it first. They're very helpful.

2. If an item has only bad reviews, it **should** / **must** not be good.

3. You probably **shouldn't** / **can't** buy the item if most of the reviews are negative.

4. If an item has several good reviews, it **can't** / **could** be worth buying.

5. Even if the reviews are positive, you still **have to** / **shouldn't** be careful.

6. When you read the reviews, you **should** / **can't** do it carefully. Make sure the reviewers are unbiased.

7. If all the reviews are great, they **might** / **can't** be reviews written by employees of the company.

8. Unless you know the source, you **may** / **can't** always trust what you read.

2 Unscramble the sentences about the rules for submitting an online review.

1. include your name / you / If you / submit a review, / must

   If you submit a review, you must include your name.

2. could / write a review, / If you / it / help other people

   _____

3. We / publish your review / if you / can't / don't include your name

   _____

4. has to / write a review for us, / be fewer than 100 words long / When you / it

   _____

5. should / you are not biased / if / Your review / include positive and negative feedback

_____

6. these rules / write a review, / When you / follow

_____

3 Look at the pictures. Then complete the real conditionals in the reviews. Use modals or modal-like expressions with the verbs in the boxes. Sometimes more than one answer is possible.

☆ ☆ ☆

~~be careful~~	decide	find	not buy

Good but Dangerous

by Ned Chapple

Overall, this meat slicer is great. However, if you buy it you

ought to be careful OR _should be careful_ . It is very sharp. If
(1)

you have children, you _____ it. However, it
(2)

does work very well. You _____ the product
(3)

very useful if you cut a lot of meat. In fact, it works so well that you

_____ to throw away your knives!
(4)

☆ ☆ ☆ ☆ ☆

download	own	save	stop buying

Reading, Even Better

by Sheila Aitchison

If you love to read, you _____ this
(5)

e-reader! It's easy to use, and you can fit a lot of books on it. If you

don't have much room at home, you _____
(6)

large, heavy books. Imagine the space you'll save! If you want to get

books quickly, you _____ books in a matter
(7)

of minutes. Books for the e-reader are often less expensive, so you

_____ money, too.
(8)

☆

be	not get	not waste	improve

Magazine Attack

by Dan Brezinsky

You _____ this magazine rack if

  (9)

you want a product that works! It's terrible. If the design is

improved, it _____ a useful product.

  (10)

As it is, it's hard to put together, and it doesn't hold many

magazines. The sellers _____ the product

  (11)

if they want to get fewer customer complaints and returns. You

_____ your money on this low-quality

  (12)

product.

be	not use	read	take up

A Good Buy

by Doris Searby

☆ ☆ ☆ ☆

This is a great lamp, but if you are very concerned about

the environment, you _____ it. You

  (13)

can't use energy-efficient bulbs with it. It only takes regular

light bulbs. It is also very big. If you have a small desk, the

lamp _____ too much room on it. It

  (14)

_____ OK for you if you have a large desk. It

  (15)

is very attractive though, and it gives off a lot of light. If you are not

sure that this is the lamp for you, you _____

  (16)

reviews of smaller, more environmentally-friendly lamps.

Avoid Common Mistakes

1 Circle the mistakes.

1. If you have a **smartphone, you** can get news updates on your phone. You can read the
   (a)
   news **quickly if** you get it on your phone. If you read an interesting news (story you) can
   (b)   (c)
   forward it to a friend.

2. **If you will want to be** a reporter, you will probably study journalism. **If you plan to be**
   (a)   (b)
   a photojournalist, you will learn to use a camera. **If you intend to be an editor**, you will
   (c)
   need to be good at grammar.

3. If you don't read the newspaper, **how do you get** news? If you don't have a computer,
   (a)
   where you will read news stories? If you have a smartphone, **do you use** it to get
   (b)   (c)
   news?

4. **If** the newspaper comes late tomorrow, I'll read it when I get home from work. **If** the
   (a)   (b)
   newspaper comes on time, I'll read it during breakfast. **When** it snows a lot tomorrow,
   (c)
   my newspaper won't be delivered at all.

5. If I help you with the article you're writing, **will you make** your deadline? If your editor
   (a)
   really likes your article, **it will be** published tomorrow? If your article is published,
   (b)
   will your parents buy several copies of the magazine?
   (c)

6. If people use social networking **sites they** sometimes post articles online. I often
   (a)
   include news **articles when** I post information online. Whenever I post something
   (b)
   interesting, my friends read the stories.
   (c)

7. It may rain, but **when** it's sunny tomorrow, we'll go to the parade. We'll take photos **if**
   (a)   (b)
   we see anything interesting. We'll submit a photo to the school newspaper **if** we get a
   (c)
   good one at tomorrow's parade.

8. If **you take** a photo of an accident, send it to the police. If **the police get** the photo, it
   (a)   (b)
   will help them find out facts about the accident. The police analysts will study the photo
   carefully if **they will get** it.
   (c)

2 Find and correct the mistakes in the article about reading news on a smartphone.

News to Go

One way to get news is to get it on your cell phone. If people are on the go, they like

to read the news wherever they are. If they have smartphones with Internet service they

can usually read news anywhere. News companies are trying to make it even easier to

get news on phones. If they will make news even easier to read on a small screen, more

5 people will read it.

Companies consider several questions when they develop stories for cell phones. For

example, if a story is long, people will read it? If people only will want to read stories on

certain topics, how people can get these stories easily?

If you will read or listen to the news on your phone, there could be some problems.

10 For example, imagine you are outside during your lunch break tomorrow, and you want

to catch up on the news. When the weather is bad tomorrow, you probably won't get

good cell phone service. You definitely won't use your phone outside when it rains a lot

tomorrow. Of course, you wouldn't read a newspaper in the rain, either!

Self-Assessment

Circle the word or phrase that correctly completes each sentence.

1. If you _____ the weather report, you will know what to wear tomorrow.

   a. will watch   b. watch   c. watching

2. If I _____ the news at 5:00, I watch the news at 7:00.

   a. will miss   b. missed   c. miss

3. Megan watches the news _____ her favorite reporter is on TV.

   a. whenever   b. unless   c. even if

4. If you always read the same _____ get different views on issues.

   a. news magazine,   b. news magazine   c. news magazine then
      you won't   you won't   you won't

5. If a newspaper often prints sensational stories, _____ it?

   a. you read   b. do you read   c. you do read

6. If a citizen journalist writes a good story, _____ it has a chance of being used by a news organization.

   a. then   b. when   c. will

7. If you tell the truth, you _____ a problem.

   a. must have   b. had   c. won't have

8. If Diane quits writing for the magazine, _____ ?

   a. what she will do   b. what will she do   c. she will do

9. _____ the reporting gets better, I won't read that online news site again.

   a. Unless   b. If   c. When

10. If she's wearing a press badge, she _____ be a reporter.

    a. will   b. can't   c. must

11. My sister believes everything she reads _____ I tell her a story is not true.

    a. then   b. even if   c. if

12. If you read Jared's article, you _____ change your mind about the new economic policies. I did.

    a. can't   b. could   c. must

13. He shouldn't submit the _____ he hasn't checked the facts. He can't rely only on his sources.

    a. article, whenever   b. article, if   c. article when

14. If you want to be a reporter, _____ take journalism classes.

    a. you won't   b. you should   c. unless you

15. If my boss calls, _____ her I'm interviewing someone for my article.

    a. tell   b. should tell   c. will tell

Unreal Conditionals: Present, Future, and Past

Natural Disasters

Present and Future Unreal Conditionals

1 Complete the unreal conditionals with the verbs in parentheses. Use the simple past in the *if* clause. Use *would* in the main clause if it is a predicted result or *might* if it is a possible result. Use the information at the end of the sentences to help you.

Brian: If there <u>*were*</u> (be) a blizzard, I <u>*wouldn't go*</u> (not go) to work. (*predicted result*)
(1)   (2)

Chris: If we _____ (have) a blizzard, we _____ (stay) home.
                 (3)   (4)
(*predicted result*)

Mark: If the city _____ (get) more than fifteen inches of snow, the mayor
                              (5)
_____ (close) the schools. (*predicted result*)
        (6)

Peter: If we _____ (not have) school, Matt _____ (catch up)
                 (7)   (8)
on his homework. (*possible result*)

Gary: If schools _____ (close), we _____ (not finish) our
                    (9)   (10)
group project in time. (*possible result*)

Paula: Claudia and Robert _____ (not drive) to the concert if there
                                (11)
_____ (be) a lot of snow on the roads. (*predicted result*)
        (12)

2 Read the information in the chart. Then write unreal conditionals about the results of the natural disasters. Use *would* to express a predicted result. Use *could* to express a possible result. Sometimes more than one answer is possible.

If Clause (condition)	Main Clause (result)	Result
1. there / be / an earthquake	buildings / fall	Possible
2. the forest fire / come / near town	residents / leave / their homes	Predicted
3. there / be / a tornado	people / go / to their basements	Predicted
4. it / rain / a lot	streets / flood	Possible
5. there / be / a hurricane	houses on the beach / be / in danger	Predicted
6. we / have / a heat wave	many plants / die	Possible

1. *If there were an earthquake, buildings could fall.* OR *Buildings could fall if there were an earthquake.*

2. _____

3. _____

4. _____

5. _____

6. _____

3 Read the report on a meeting about school closings. Then rewrite the quotations in bold as present unreal conditionals. Make any necessary changes in wording.

At the city board meeting on Friday, many people expressed their concerns about the number of snow days at local schools. Eric Sheffield, a concerned parent, said, **"The mayor cancels school constantly, so our students can't get a solid education."** Mayor Jenkins responded, **"It snows frequently, so I have to cancel school."** He added that if
5 more than six days are missed, they will be made up at the end of the year. Blanca Morales, a school teacher, said, **"We miss a large number of days, so we have to make them up at the end of the year."** Mayor Jenkins responded, **"Safety is a priority, so I can't keep schools open during bad weather."** Dan Park, a local businessman, mentioned that the city doesn't have enough equipment to clear all the roads for school buses. He said,
10 **"The city doesn't have good snow removal equipment, so we have a lot of canceled school days."** Melanie Brooks, a city employee, said, **"The city doesn't raise taxes, so we can't buy new equipment."** She added that people probably didn't want higher taxes. The discussion will continue at next month's meeting.

1. Eric Sheffield: *If the mayor didn't cancel school constantly, our students could get a solid education.*

2. Mayor Jenkins: _____

_____

3. Blanca Morales: _____

_____

4. Mayor Jenkins: _____

_____

5. Dan Park: _____

_____

6. Melanie Brooks: _____

_____

4 Look at the web article about things to do in Seattle and at the weather forecast for each day. Then write advice for tourists about each day of their vacation. Use present unreal conditionals. Sometimes more than one answer is possible.

Things to Do in Seattle

- Take a city bus tour
- Hike Mount Rainier – Amazing volcano just 60 miles from the city
- Visit the Space Needle – Fantastic city views from the top on a clear day
- Take a ferry to the San Juan Islands – Beautiful wildlife just an hour from
5   Anacortes, which is about 80 miles from Seattle
- Go to the Museum of Flight – Entertainment and information for the entire family
- Shop at Pike Place Market – This indoor market has been selling the best local food for over 100 years
10 • Take an underground tour of Pioneer Square – A very interesting and unusual view of the city and its history

1. Monday

   If I were you, I wouldn't visit the Space Needle. OR *I would go to the Museum of Flight if I were you.*

2. Tuesday

   _____

3. Wednesday

   _____

4. Thursday

   _____

5. Friday

   _____

Past Unreal Conditionals

1 Read the sentences about a fire. Then answer the *Yes / No* questions.

1. If there hadn't been a heat wave, the fire wouldn't have started.

   a. Was there a heat wave? _Yes_

   b. Was there a fire? _Yes_

2. If the firefighters hadn't responded quickly, the fire would have spread to other buildings.

   a. Did the firefighters respond quickly? _____

   b. Did the fire spread to more than one building? _____

3. No one would have been injured if everyone had left the area.

   a. Did everyone leave the area? _____

   b. Was anyone injured? _____

4. Two people could have died if they hadn't been rescued in time by the firefighters.

   a. Were the people rescued in time? _____

   b. Did anyone die? _____

5. If the fire hadn't occurred during the day, a lot of people might have been injured.

   a. Did the fire occur during the day? _____

   b. Were a lot of people injured? _____

2 Rewrite the sentences about the 2010 eruption of a volcano in Iceland. Use *if* to make past unreal conditionals.

1. Most people heard about the eruption because it disrupted a lot of flights.

   Most people wouldn't have heard about the eruption if it hadn't disrupted a lot of flights.

2. Flights didn't continue because the smoke and ash were so thick in the air.

   _____

3. Flights stopped because the pilots weren't able to see.

   _____

4. Many tourists didn't fly home because the airports closed.

   _____

5. The catastrophe affected so many countries in Europe because the wind was so strong.

   _____

3 Look at the picture of a street after a storm. Then complete the past unreal conditionals. Use the verbs in the box. In the main clause, use *would* for predicted results and *could* or *might* for possible results. Sometimes more than one answer is possible.

be	~~fall~~	not get	remember	slow
close	go	not step	see	stay

1. The trash can _might not have fallen_ over if it _had been_ heavier.

2. If the driver _____ down, Alison

   _____ dry.

3. The car seats _____ wet if Bobby

   _____ the windows.

4. If Melissa _____ the puddle, she

   _____ in it.

5. The dogs _____ inside if someone

   _____ to let them in.

4 Complete the conversation about what people did during a thunderstorm. Write indirect advice using past unreal conditionals. Write sentences that are true for you.

1. **A:** The power went out, and I sat in the dark for four hours!

   B: _____

2. **A:** I talked on my cell phone until the battery died.

   B: _____

3. **A:** I assumed the food in the refrigerator would stay fresh.

   B: _____

4. **A:** I went to bed and left the windows open.

   B: _____

5. **A:** I left some candles burning while I slept.

   B: _____

Wishes About the Present, Future, and Past

1 Complete the phone conversation. Use the simple past, past progressive, past perfect, *would*, or *could* with the verbs in parentheses.

Annie: I wish that I <u>*had seen*</u> (see) the tornado yesterday.
(1)

Jorge: I saw it while I was driving.

Annie: Really? That must have been scary.

Jorge: It was. I wish I _____ (be) home during the tornado. But I'm
(2)

glad that I got home OK after it passed.

Annie: This weather has been crazy. I wish that it _____ (not rain) now.
(3)

Jorge: I know. I don't want to drive in this weather. I wish I _____ (not make)
(4)

plans to go out today.

Annie: Can you cancel them?

Jorge: No. I have an interview this afternoon. I wish I _____ (reschedule)
(5)

it, but I can't.

Annie: What job are you interviewing for?

Jorge: It's for a disaster recovery organization. I'd be answering phones. I wish that it

_____ (be) a better job, but it's a start.
(6)

Annie: Yes . . . you need to start somewhere. Then maybe you can get a promotion. I wish

my boss _____ (promote) me, but she won't.
    (7)

Jorge: Could you ask her for a raise?

Annie: I wish that I _____ (ask) for a raise, but my company isn't giving
    (8)

raises this year. Maybe next year. . . .

Jorge: Yes. It's good to have a positive attitude. Well, I wish I _____ (talk)
    (9)

longer, but I can't. I need to get ready for my interview.

Annie: OK. Good luck. Call me back after the interview!

2 Write sentences with *wish* to express the people's wishes and regrets.

1. I didn't take any pictures of the storm.

   I wish (that) I had taken pictures of the storm.

2. I left my umbrella at home.

   _____

3. I can't go outside and play soccer right now.

   _____

4. I hope the rain stops.

   _____

5. It rains every week here. I don't like it.

   _____

6. My rain boots have holes in them.

   _____

7. I can't go to the park today.

   _____

8. I like the winter. Then it snows.

   _____

Avoid Common Mistakes

1 Circle the mistakes.

1. If Paul **didn't work** with disaster relief, he wouldn't be so stressed. Also, if he (**works**)
     (a)   (b)

   fewer hours, he would spend more time with friends. I really think that he would have

   more time in the day if he **got** a different job.
                                 (c)

2. We would watch TV **if the power were working**. We could listen to the radio **if had**
                          (a)   (b)

   batteries. **If our phone were working**, we would call our family to say we are OK.
              (c)

3. Our office would have been destroyed if the architect **didn't design** it to withstand
                                                             (a)

   earthquakes. I wish all the buildings in our city **had been built** as well as ours was. But
                                                       (b)

   they were not. If the earthquake **had been** bigger, a lot of buildings would have fallen.
                                       (c)

4. I wish you **had seen** the storm. It was amazing! If I **charged** my camera batteries,
                (a)   (b)

   I **could have taken** pictures to show you.
      (c)

5. If he **trained** better, he could have passed the test. If he **had passed** the test, he would
          (a)   (b)

   have been a firefighter. His parents would have been proud if he **had become**
                                                                        (c)

   a firefighter.

6. If we **worked** together, we could make a difference. We could raise a lot of money if we
          (a)

   chose to work for the same charity. I would love it if we **work** together for survivors of
    (b)   (c)

   the hurricane.

7. I wish you **called** me. If you **had told** me about the storm, I **would have come and stayed**
                 (a)   (b)   (c)

   with you.

8. **A:** If **I were** you, I would take an umbrella to work today.
            (a)

   B: I hate when it rains. It would be great if **I could leave** work early.
                                                       (b)

   A: If **you get** to work on time every day, it might be easier to leave early.
            (c)

2 Find and correct eight more mistakes in the article about a survivor of a blizzard.

Joe Simpson: Survivor

      weren't
If it ~~isn't~~ for a tragic event, no one would know about Joe Simpson. In 1985, Joe

Simpson and Simon Yates were climbing a mountain in the Andes. If a blizzard didn't

happen, the trip might have ended without any problems. The two climbers got to the

top of the mountain, but they had problems on the way down. If it hadn't been icy, Joe

5 wouldn't have slipped. However, it was icy, and Joe slipped and broke his leg. He could

have climbed down the mountain if hadn't gotten the injury. Because Joe couldn't walk,

Simon lowered Joe down the mountain on a rope. When they were almost back to the

camp, Joe slipped again. He was dangling on the rope over the edge of the mountain. He

could have climbed up the rope if had had the strength. If the weather didn't damage

10 Simon's hands, he might have been able to pull Joe up. Simon held on to the rope for

several hours, but he finally had to cut the rope. He thought Joe had died, but Joe was not

dead. He had fallen more than 100 feet, but even with his hurt leg, he had managed to

climb to safety and get back to the camp.

      In 1988, Joe Simpson wrote a book, called *Touching the Void*, about the experience. If

15 the book wasn't a huge success, the movie about the climb might not have been made. I

wish that I did not see the movie before I read the book. I also wish I went to the movie

with a friend. It was frightening! Of course, it was inspiring, too. If I am you, I would rent

the movie today!

Self-Assessment

Circle the word or phrase that correctly completes each sentence.

1. If I _____ how to ski, I would go skiing with you.

    a. know   b. had known   c. knew

2. If the roads weren't icy, I _____ worry about driving to work.

    a. didn't   b. wouldn't   c. could

3. She wouldn't go to school if she _____ sick.

   a. were   b. is   c. be

4. If it hadn't been so hot, the fire might not _____ .

   a. started   b. start   c. have started

5. I wouldn't go outside if I _____ you.

   a. could be   b. were   c. am

6. If the storm had been reported on the news, we _____ for it.

   a. are ready   b. might get ready   c. might have been ready

7. If it had snowed more, the city _____ the schools.

   a. closed   b. would have closed   c. would close

8. I _____ you about the storm if my phone had worked.

   a. will tell   b. would have told   c. told

9. If I hadn't been nervous, I _____ better during the interview.

   a. could have done   b. could do   c. did do

10. If I _____ you, I would have stayed in the basement during the storm.

    a. was   b. am   c. had been

11. If I _____ the training, I could have become a firefighter.

    a. had finished   b. have finished   c. could finish

12. I _____ that it would snow.

    a. wishing   b. wish   c. would wish

13. Janet wishes that she _____ her umbrella at home this morning.

    a. isn't leaving   b. didn't leave   c. hadn't left

14. I wish we _____ better disaster policies in our state. Can't our legislators do something about it?

    a. were having   b. have   c. had

15. Hai wishes he _____ snowboard. He wants to learn how.

    a. could   b. would   c. might

Conjunctions
Globalization of Food

Connecting Words and Phrases with Conjunctions

1 A Look at the menu. Then complete the sentences. Use *and* or *or*. Sometimes more than one answer is possible.

Dinner Special

Choose one entrée and two sides.
Dinner also comes with a small salad or soup, a drink, and a dessert.

Entrées

Meat: chicken, beef, lamb

Fish: salmon, tuna, shrimp

Vegetarian: eggplant, tofu

Sides

Potatoes: baked potato, French fries

Vegetables: corn, carrots, peas

Drinks

coffee, tea, soda

Dessert

chocolate cake, apple pie

1. For the dinner special, you can choose one entrée _*and*_ two sides.

2. You can choose a small salad _____ soup with the dinner special.

3. The dinner special comes with a drink _____ a dessert.

4. For the entrée, you can have meat, fish, _____ a vegetarian dish.

5. The eggplant _____ the tofu are vegetarian dishes.

6. For a side, you can choose a potato _____ a vegetable dish.

7. Coffee, tea, _____ soda are all drinks on the menu.

8. For dessert, you can choose the chocolate cake _____ the apple pie.

B Look at the menu in A again. Then complete the restaurant review. Use *and*, *but*, or *or*. Sometimes more than one answer is possible.

The restaurant Mango opened last month. The restaurant is spacious <u>*and*</u> modern. The
(1)
restaurant is new _____ already popular. You need to call for reservations.
(2)

The food is inexpensive _____ delicious. The dinner special is the best value for
(3)
your money. It comes with an entrée, a small salad or soup, two sides, a drink, _____
(4)
a dessert. For the entrée, try the chicken _____ the eggplant. The chicken is really
(5)
spicy _____ not too peppery. The eggplant is mild _____ still tasty. Don't try the
(6)   (7)
beef, the lamb, _____ the tuna. They're all overcooked. The one item you must have is
(8)
the chocolate cake. It's chocolaty _____ not too sweet!
(9)

2 Complete the conversation between a waiter and a customer. Use *and*, *but also*, *nor*, or *or* with the simple present form of the verbs in parentheses.

Waiter: Can I take your order, or do you have any questions about the menu?

Customer: Yes. Do you recommend the salmon or the tuna?

Waiter: Both the salmon <u>*and*</u> the tuna <u>*are*</u> (be) delicious.
(1)   (2)

Customer: Are they salty?

Waiter: No. Neither the salmon _____ the tuna _____ (be) salty.
(3)   (4)

Customer: Well, I guess I'll have the tuna with a salad.

Waiter: Do you want the Greek salad or the house salad?

Customer: Either the Greek salad _____ the house salad _____ (be) fine. Which do you
(5)   (6)
recommend?

Waiter: I prefer the Greek salad. As the menu says, "Not only the dressing _____ the cheese
(7)
_____ (add) to the taste of this customer favorite."
(8)

Customer: OK. That sounds good.

Waiter: Great. Do you want French fries or a baked potato?

Customer: To be honest, neither the French fries _____ the baked potato _____ (sound)
(9)   (10)
good. Can I get something healthier?

Waiter: How about a vegetable? Both the corn _____ the carrots _____ (be) healthy.
(11)   (12)

Customer: I'll have the corn. Thanks.

3 Combine the sentences about two restaurants that serve *crêpes*, a kind of thin pancake. Use the correlative conjunctions in parentheses. Sometimes more than one answer is possible.

1. La Crêperie is a restaurant that serves crêpes. Sweet Spot is a restaurant that serves crêpes. (both . . . and)

   Both La Crêperie and Sweet Spot are restaurants that serve crêpes.

2. At the restaurants, you can have savory crêpes. At the restaurants, you can have sweet crêpes. (either . . . or)

   _____

3. The crêpes are inexpensive. They are large. (not only . . . but also)

   _____

4. The chocolate crêpes are delicious. The strawberry crêpes are delicious. (both . . . and)

   _____

5. Coffee is not free at La Crêperie. Tea is not free at La Crêperie. (neither . . . nor)

   _____

Connecting Sentences with Coordinating Conjunctions

1 Complete the paragraphs about a cooking show. Use *and*, *but*, or *so*. Only use *and* when no other conjunction is possible. Sometimes more than one answer is possible.

The Globalization of TV

Iron Chef was a TV show in Japan, _**and**_ it was very popular in the 1990s. On the show,
                                      (1)
two chefs would compete in each episode. One chef was an Iron Chef, the name given to

the chefs who were on the show repeatedly. The other chef was a guest chef. Both the Iron

Chef and the guest chef were given a type of food, _____ they had to make dishes
                                                        (2)
with that food as the main ingredient. The chefs usually used the main ingredient in four

dishes, _____ they sometimes cooked five or more dishes. The show was only an
         (3)
hour long, _____ the chefs didn't have much time to cook, _____ each of them
            (4)   (5)
was helped by two assistants. Then judges ate the food. One of the judges was usually a

professional food critic, _____ the other judges were often just celebrities. The judges
                           (6)
scored the food, _____ the chef with the highest points won the competition.
                  (7)

Iron Chef ended in Japan in 1999, _____ reruns of the show were played in the
(8)
United States. The Japanese show became popular in the United States, _____ a U.S.
(9)
version called *Iron Chef America* was developed in 2005.

2 Complete the sentences about Mexican food. Circle the correct conjunctions.

1. Authentic Mexican food has a lot of spices, (**yet**)/ **and** it doesn't always taste very spicy.

2. There are some really spicy sauces, **but / and** they're not served with every dish.

3. Danielle loves cheese, **or / so** cheese enchiladas are her favorite dish.

4. Some diners always have enchiladas with a red sauce, **yet / so** it is possible to get them with a green sauce, too.

5. In Mexico, the beef tacos usually have shredded beef, **yet / or** they're made with steak.

6. In some Mexican restaurants in the United States and Canada, the food is quite different from the food served in Mexico, **yet / and** it is still advertised as Mexican.

3 Read the article about international food. Rewrite these sentences with a compound verb. In some sentences, the subject or the subject + auxiliary verb does not need to be repeated.

➷ International Food ❧

Many cuisines are popular around the world. Look at our list of some of the most popular types of food around the world.

◈ There are many Greek restaurants around the world, and they are often owned by Greek people.

5 ◈ Chinese food is eaten everywhere, and it is our number-one choice for international food.

◈ Mexican food is popular, and it is enjoyed by people in many countries.

◈ Thai food can be found in many places, and it is usually similar to the food in Thailand.

◈ Italian food is found around the world, but the pizza is better in Italy!

10 ◈ Indian restaurants are common in England, and they are found in many other countries.

◈ You should try French food in France, and you should have it in Canada.

◈ Japanese restaurants are in many countries, and sushi is often on the menu.

1. *Chinese food is eaten everywhere and is our number-one choice for*
   international food.

2. _____

3. _____

4. _____

5. _____

Reducing Sentences with Similar Clauses

1 Complete the online message board comments about chain restaurants. Use the correct verb forms. Add *too*, *so*, *either*, or *neither* when necessary.

Jake07: I want to know what you think! Should people eat at American chain restaurants when they travel to other countries?

Dond27: No way! Chain restaurants are terrible in the United States, and the chain restaurants in other countries _are_ , _too_ .

(1)   (1)

Maria52: I disagree. The quality of chain restaurant food in the United States is good and dependable, and it _____ in Mexico, _____ !

(2)   (2)

SG1987: I agree with Dond27. I haven't had good food in chain restaurants here, and I _____ in other countries _____ .

(3)   (3)

TOOTIE: I'm with Maria52. I ate at a pizza chain in India. The pizza was terrific, and _____ _____ the atmosphere!

(4)   (4)

KVN67: I agree with Maria52, too. Once I ate at a fast-food restaurant in Switzerland. The burger was fantastic, and the potatoes _____, _____ . The

(5)   (5)

burger was fried, but the potatoes _____ . I think the potatoes were

(6)

baked. Good . . . and healthy!

Friendlee: Last year, I ate at a burger restaurant in France. The burger wasn't good, but the fries _____ . In fact, the fries were delicious!

(7)

G3Harris: I don't want to eat at chain restaurants when I travel, and _____

(8)

_____ my family! We like to try the local food.

(8)

Rita2010: I'm with G3Harris. I won't even eat in chain restaurants here in the United States, and my husband _____ _____ !

(9)   (9)

Jake07: Thanks, everyone. I'm enjoying reading your opinions, and _____ _____

(10)   (10)

my roommates! Please keep posting.

2 Read a restaurant critic's rating chart about the main courses available in a restaurant. Then write two sentences for each statement. Use *too*, *so*, *either*, or *neither* with the words in parentheses.

	Expensive	Grilled	Good	Salty
Chicken	No	No	Yes	Yes
Steak	Yes	Yes	Yes	No
Lamb	Yes	No	No	No
Fish	No	Yes	No	Yes

1. The chicken isn't expensive.

   (fish)   *Neither is the fish.*   *The fish isn't, either.*

2. The steak is expensive.

   (lamb)   _____   _____

3. The lamb isn't grilled.

   (chicken)   _____   _____

4. The fish is grilled.

   (steak)   _____   _____

5. The chicken was good.

   (steak)   _____   _____

6. The lamb wasn't good.

   (fish)   _____   _____

7. The steak wasn't salty.

   (lamb)   _____   _____

8. The fish was salty.

   (chicken)   _____   _____

3 Write sentences about restaurants with information that is true for you. Use two clauses and reduce the words in the second clause. Use *too*, *so*, *either*, *neither*, or *but*.

1. Burger restaurants / be / popular

   _____

2. I / like / French food

   _____

3. I / eat / fast food

_____

4. Italian food / be / popular

_____

5. Sushi / be / popular

_____

6. Salad bars / be / healthy

_____

7. Many people / don't like / spicy foods

_____

Avoid Common Mistakes

1 Circle the mistakes.

1. The restaurant serves Mexican **and** Central American food. It doesn't have TexMex food
   (a)
   and food from Spain. You can't get *chili con carne* **or** *paella.*
   (b)   (c)

2. Jorge wants to open **a restaurant, and he'd** like it to be downtown. He'll serve food
   (a)
   in **the restaurant and have** a take-out service. He plans to borrow money from
   (b)
   his parents, and pay them back.
   (c)

3. The United States has a lot of Chinese restaurants, and Costa Rica does, **too**. The
   (a)
   American restaurants don't always have traditional food from China, and the Costa
   Rican restaurants don't, **too**. The Americans have adapted some of the dishes, and the
   (b)
   Costa Ricans have, **too**.
   (c)

4. **Either** Italian food and French food are popular in the United States. Some Italian
   (a)
   restaurants serve **both** authentic Italian dishes and Italian-American dishes. Some
   (b)
   French restaurants serve **either** standard French dishes or dishes from different regions
   (c)
   in France.

5. Bob's Pizza serves Americanized pizza, and Andy's does, **too.** Traditional Italian
   (a)
   pizza doesn't have a thick red sauce, and it doesn't have thick melted cheese, **either.**
   (b)
   Traditional Italian pizza doesn't have a chewy crust, and the crust isn't thick, **too.**
   (c)

6. A *churrascaria* is a traditional Brazilian restaurant that is popular in **both** Brazil and the
   (a)
   United States. These restaurants have **either** a salad bar and all-you-can-eat meat. You
   (b)
   usually have a card at your table that you can turn to **either** red (stop serving) or green
   (c)
   (keep serving).

7. In my town, there isn't a Greek restaurant **and** a Thai one. We also don't have a Korean
   (a)
   restaurant **or** a Japanese one. We do have a Mexican restaurant **and** a Chinese one.
   (b)   (c)

8. I love **Korean food but don't like** kimchi. It is too **spicy for me, and I don't like** the
   (a)   (b)
   flavor. Kimchi usually comes in **a separate dish, and is served** as a side.
                                    (c)

2 Find and correct seven more mistakes in the article about fruit-growing regions.

Oranges All Year Round

Places like Florida and California can grow fruit year-round, but places like New York

and Minnesota cannot because the climate is too cold. For example, oranges do not grow

$$\textit{either}$$

in cold climates, and lemons do not, ~~too~~. However, either oranges and lemons can be

found in supermarkets all year round. Where do they come from? Most supermarkets in

5 places with cold winters import food from other places. Oranges are grown in California,

and are shipped to places like New York.

There are some fruits that do not grow well in warm and cold climates in the United

States. Therefore, many fruits are imported from other countries. For example, either

Peru and Mexico export avocados to the United States. Durian is not native to the United

10 States, and passion fruit is not, too. Durian is often imported from Malaysia and Indonesia,

and passion fruit is imported from New Zealand and Brazil. Lychee is another fruit that is

not very common in the United States. It is grown in some areas of the United States, but

is mainly imported from places like China. These exotic fruits usually cannot be found in

small towns and smaller cities. However, supermarkets in bigger cities usually sell them.

Self-Assessment

Circle the word or phrase that correctly completes each sentence.

1. I love to eat exotic fruits and _____ .

    a. vegetables   b. delicious   c. buy

2. Do you want to go to an Italian restaurant _____ a French restaurant for dinner?

    a. and   b. or   c. but

3. My local supermarket, which is owned by some Greek immigrants, imports fruit from Asia, Africa, _____ South America.

    a. and   b. or   c. but

4. Durian tastes delicious _____ smells awful.

    a. and   b. or   c. but

5. _____ mangoes and lychee are grown in India.

    a. Not only   b. Either   c. Both

6. Neither passion fruit nor oranges _____ in this area.

    a. grow   b. grows   c. to grow

7. This restaurant serves _____ traditional and adapted Korean dishes.

    a. both   b. either   c. neither

8. Durian is prickly on the outside, _____ the inside is soft.

    a. yet   b. or   c. nor

9. Our town is located near Mexico, _____ we cross the border to eat at authentic Mexican restaurants.

    a. or   b. but   c. so

10. We could order _____ get pasta.

    a. pizza so   b. pizza or   c. pizza, or

11. My sister loves _____ I don't like it.

    a. lychee, or   b. lychee and   c. lychee, but

12. My parents don't like to try food from other cultures, but I _____ .

    a. don't   b. do   c. neither

13. Chinese food is delicious, and _____ Chinese-American food.

    a. either is   b. so is   c. neither is

14. I have tried durian, and my brother _____ .

    a. too   b. has, too   c. hasn't, either

15. Paul doesn't drink coffee after a meal, and _____ .

    a. neither do I   b. I do neither   c. neither don't I

Adverb Clauses and Phrases

Consumerism

Subordinators and Adverb Clauses

1 Complete the article about saving money. Circle the correct subordinators.

I decided to find ways to save money **though** /(**because**)I was spending too much and
(1)
having financial problems. You may find these tips helpful **while / since** they worked
(2)
for me!

- I take a list with me **while / because** I'm shopping, and I buy only the items on the list.
  (3)
- I opened up a savings account. **Although / As** I had a checking account, I had never
  (4)
  had a savings account. Now I put money in it every month. **Even though / Since** I do
  (5)
  not put a lot of money in it, the money adds up over time!

- I make a monthly budget. **While / Because** I have bills to pay every month, I
  (6)
  write down what I need to spend every month on rent, food, and things like that.

  While / When it is still tempting to spend too much, I find that with a budget it is
  (7)
  easier to resist spending urges.

- I cook at home more. I love to eat out, but I have done it less often **though / since**
  (8)
  I realized I was spending too much at restaurants. I also take my lunch to work.

- I use a small part of my savings to go shopping once a month. **While / As** before I
  (9)
  would waste money throughout the month, now I buy one item for myself at the end
  of the month.

  Good luck! I hope you can save money **even though / as** it's rewarding in the end!
  (10)

2 Look at the chart about how Americans spend money. Then complete the sentences with adverb clauses. Use the subordinators *although*, *because*, *even though*, *since*, *though*, *when*, or *while* with the correct percentages. Sometimes more than one answer is possible.

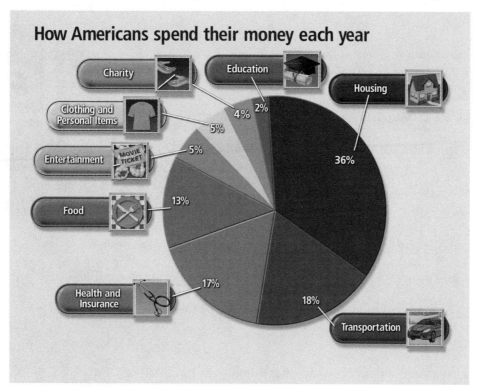

How Americans spend their money each year

Charity   Education   Housing

Clothing and Personal Items

Entertainment   MOVIE TICKET

Food

Health and Insurance

Transportation

4%   2%

5%

5%

13%

36%

17%

18%

http://www.bls.gov/opub/focus/volume2_number12/cex_2_12.htm

1. _*Although* OR *Even though* OR *Though*_ Americans spend _36_ percent of their money on housing, only 60 percent of that money is for rent or mortgage payment. The rest is spent on things like heating and cooling the home.

2. _____ Americans spend _____ percent of their money on transportation, only 34 percent of that money is for the price of a car. The rest is for gas or other kinds of transportation, like buses.

3. Health and insurance are inexpensive in other countries, _____ Americans spend _____ percent of their money on health and insurance.

4. _____ Americans spend _____ percent of their money on food, about half of that money is not spent on groceries, but instead on eating out.

5. _____ they shop, both in stores and online, Americans spend _____ percent of their money on clothing and personal items.

6. We can probably consider Americans fairly generous _____ they give _____ percent of their money to charities.

Reducing Adverb Clauses

1 Read the article about personal shoppers. Then rewrite the clauses in bold as reduced clauses.

Christina is a personal shopper who works for a
businesswoman, Mrs. Adams. *Being very busy* ~~Because she is very busy~~,

Mrs. Adams does not have time to shop. Christina does most

of her shopping. **Since she is a successful businesswoman,**

5 Mrs. Adams often has to go to events. Christina picks out

dresses and shoes for her. Christina also gets groceries

for Mrs. Adams. **While she gets Mrs. Adams groceries**, Christina also does her

own shopping. Christina started working for Mrs. Adams **after she started college**.

Because she has earned enough money for her tuition, Christina will finish school

10 this year.

David is also a personal shopper, but his job is different from Christina's. David

goes shopping for elderly people. **Because they are homebound**, his clients have

difficulty leaving their houses. David does their grocery shopping and also buys other

items for them. One of his clients, Mr. Morton, said that David has changed his life.

15 **Since he had a stroke two years ago**, Mr. Morton has had trouble walking. His children

did his shopping for him **before they realized a service could do it**. Now when they visit

their father, they can spend time with him instead of doing errands for him.

2 Rewrite the sentences. Use reduced clauses.

1. Because she is a "shoe addict," Melissa buys more shoes than she needs.

   Being a "shoe addict," Melissa buys more shoes than she needs.

2. Because she had bought 100 pairs of shoes, she didn't have room for them in her closet.

   _____

3. While she was shopping for a gift for her sister, she bought three new pairs of shoes.

   _____

4. She started buying shoes before she got a job.

   _____

5. Because they are caring people, her parents were worried about her.

    _____

6. Because he had read an article about shopping addicts, her father suggested treatment.

    _____

7. Melissa agreed to get help after she realized she had a problem.

    _____

8. Now she takes only the money she needs when she goes to the mall.

    _____

3 Write sentences about your own shopping habits, preferences, or experiences for each topic. Use reduced clauses with information that is true for you.

1. (malls) _____ .

2. (shoes) _____ .

3. (gifts) _____ .

4. (online shopping) _____ .

5. (clothes) _____ .

Subordinators to Express Purpose

1 Complete the conversations. Circle the correct subordinators.

A Yae Won: Hi, Aaron. What are you doing at the mall?

    Aaron: I need a new suit **in order to** /(**so that**) I can look professional for my job
                           (1)
            interview. What are you doing here?

    Yae Won: I came here **so** / **to** get a birthday present for my sister.
                              (2)

B Franco: Hey, Paul, did you ever buy that thing you needed **so that** / **to** fix your lamp?
                                          (3)

    Paul: No. It was almost as expensive as a new lamp! I bought a new lamp instead

           in order to / **so** I don't have to deal with fixing it.
              (4)

C **Isabel:** Can you believe Doug bought a new car? He's always buying things

in order to / so that feel important.

(5)

Ahmed: Well, some people buy new things **so that / to** they can feel good. But I don't

(6)

think that's the case with Doug.

D **Nina:** I have too much stuff! I'm having a sale **in order to / so** I can get rid of some of

(7)

my things. Do you want to help me?

Vicky: OK. But are you sure you aren't selling your stuff **so that / to** buy new things?

(8)

2 Look at the chart about what people buy and why. Then write sentences with the information in the chart and the words in parentheses.

Who	Purchase	Why
1. Melissa	shoes	It makes her feel good.
2. Santiago	old guitars	He can fix them.
3. Dae Jin and Alex	concert tickets	They want to sell them to their friends.
4. Gabriela	new clothes	She can have the latest style.
5. Chuck	comic books	He likes to add them to his collection.
6. Sofia and Ying	art supplies	They can make birthday cards to sell.

1. (in order to) _Melissa buys shoes in order to feel good._

2. (so that) _____

3. (to) _____

4. (so) _____

5. (in order to) _____

6. (so that) _____

3 Write sentences about the reason why you buy each type of item. Use subordinators with the words in parentheses. Write sentences that are true for you.

1. (electronics) _____

2. (books) _____

3. (gifts) _____

4. (music) _____

Avoid Common Mistakes

1 Circle the mistakes.

1. **Although** it's a holiday, the stores are open. **Even though** it is almost 10:00 p.m., I'm
   (a)   (b)
   still shopping. I'll buy something for myself, (**eventhough**) I need to get my sister a gift.
                                                   (c)

2. We're going shopping **because** I need a suit. I need you to help me. **Because** I don't
                        (a)   (b)
   know what looks good. **Because** I don't have a lot of money, I need to find something
                          (c)
   on sale.

3. Americans spend more on health care than Canadians **because** Canada's government
                                                        (a)
   provides more coverage. **Being** Canadian, I prefer our health care system. After **get**
                            (b)   (c)
   sick last year, I didn't have to pay for any of my doctor's appointments.

4. I hate shopping **even** I like to have new clothes. I really dislike shopping alone, **although**
                    (a)   (b)
   it's sometimes easier than shopping with friends. However, I have to go shopping by
   myself tomorrow **even though** I hate it.
                     (c)

5. I'm going to buy a guitar **so that** I can play in my brother's band. I'm going to take guitar
                             (a)
   lessons **eventhough** I'm already pretty good. **Though** I don't sing that much, I might
            (b)   (c)
   sing backup in the band.

6. **Because** I don't want to spend money at a restaurant, I take my lunch to work. I do,
   (a)
   however, go out to eat **when** my boss pays for lunch. She takes us out every month.
                           (b)
   Although the restaurants are expensive.
   (c)

7. I like to shop online **even though** I can't try the clothes on. Clothing online can be
                          (a)
   cheap, **though** I have to remember to pay my credit card bill later. **Even** I have to pay
           (b)   (c)
   for shipping, I usually spend less money online than in stores.

8. My roommate and I like shopping online while **watch** TV. I don't buy a lot of things,
                                                 (a)
   whereas my roommate **is** a shopping addict. After **realizing** he had a problem, he tried
                        (b)   (c)
   to stop, but he got really depressed. I think he needs to seek professional help.

2 Find and correct nine more mistakes in the article about spending patterns.

Spending Patterns

Even though
~~Even~~ everyone spends money differently, research shows there is a common pattern of

spending over a lifetime:

- From ages 18 to 22, people do not spend a lot of money. Young people often do not

  have a lot of money to spend. Because they are in school or getting their first job.

5 • People who are 22 to 30 spend a little more money. Although they still do not spend

  that much. For example, people in their 20s often cannot afford to buy houses when

  not earn a lot of money. As a result, they tend to rent apartments.

- From ages 31 to 40, people spend more money. They usually have more money to

  spend. Because they have been working for a while. However, eventhough they

10   make more money, they often have a hard time *saving* money.

- Research shows that people in their 40s spend the most money. Many people in this

  age group have children, so they have to buy things for the entire family.

- People in their 50s spend less money than those in their 40s even they often have

  more money than when they were younger. One of the reasons is that, eventhough

15   they may continue working, they are often trying to save money for retirement.

- People over 60 spend the least amount of money. Many people in this age group are

  not working anymore after have retired, so they are usually afraid of spending much

  money, even they have saved money for most of their lives.

Self-Assessment

Circle the word or phrase that correctly completes each sentence.

1. You save money on sale items _____ you get a discount.

   a. while   b. because   c. although

2. _____ he was in class, Bryan was shopping online.

   a. So   b. So that   c. While

3. _____ some shoppers save on each sale item, they buy more items than they need.

   a. To   b. Although   c. In order to

4. Tatiana doesn't mind paying full price, _____ Ivan won't buy anything if it's not on sale.

   a. while   b. as   c. since

5. Some people actually spend more money _____ they use coupons.

   a. so that   b. since   c. when

6. I was shopping online before _____ my boss was near my desk.

   a. had realized   b. realize   c. realizing

7. _____ gotten a warning, Ari stopped shopping online at work.

   a. Having   b. Being   c. Because

8. _____ a teenager, Jordan spends most of her money on clothing and entertainment.

   a. Having   b. Being   c. Because

9. While _____ , Julia was sending text messages.

   a. shopping   b. shop   c. was shopping

10. Having _____ a large phone bill, Colin's parents took his phone away.

    a. get   b. gotten   c. getting

11. Katia gave away some of her old clothes after _____ new ones.

    a. to buy   b. bought   c. buying

12. I want to buy a car _____ I don't have take the bus anymore.

    a. to   b. in order to   c. so

13. Jared usually pays for dinner _____ be generous to his friends.

    a. so   b. in order to   c. so that

14. Let's go to the new Korean restaurant early so that _____ a seat.

    a. getting   b. we can get   c. get

15. I'm going to the mall to _____ a new pair of shoes.

    a. buy   b. I buy   c. buying

Connecting Information with Prepositions and Transitions

Technology in Entertainment

Connecting Information with Prepositions and Prepositional Phrases

1 Complete the article about acting and motion capture technology. Circle the correct prepositions and prepositional phrases.

Acting may be getting more challenging for actors (**due to**)/ **besides** technology. **Instead of / Because of**
(1)   (2)
new inventions, actors need to find new methods of acting. With motion capture (mocap) technology, the actors' movements are captured and then turned into an animation. **As well as / Instead of** wearing a tight suit
(3)
that captures movement, actors in motion capture films may also wear a helmet[1] with a camera. **Instead of / Except for** acting on a realistic
(4)
set, actors act in a strange, empty room that may not have anything **due to / except for**
(5)
a large screen. These are challenges because actors often say sets and costumes help them "become" a character. **In addition to / In spite of** these challenges, an actor may
(6)
sometimes talk to a spot on the screen **instead of / despite** another character. The
(7)
character that the actor is talking to will be created later by an animator. For example, in the final movie, it may look like the actor is talking to an animated cat or a dog.

Despite / As well as the difficulties of acting with mocap technology, actors are doing
(8)
amazing work with it. The movies seem believable **in spite of / in addition to** the
(9)
unrealistic situations in which the actors perform.

---

[1]helmet: a hard hat that covers and protects the head

2 Read the conversation about going to the movies. Then complete the sentences with the words in parentheses and information from the conversation. Sometimes more than one answer is possible.

Martin: Was the movie worth seeing?

Kala: Yes, but the ticket price was high!

Martin: Did you see an animated movie?

Kala: No. I went to an action movie.

5 **Martin:** Did you get any popcorn?

Kala: Yes. I'm on a diet, but I got popcorn anyway.

Martin: Did you get anything else?

Kala: Yes! I had a soda and some chocolate!

Martin: Did you have a good time?

10 **Kala:** Well, kind of. I couldn't see the movie very well. The theater had bad seats.

Martin: Is that why you're holding your neck?

Kala: Yes! I sat too close to the screen and now my neck hurts.

1. Kala thinks the movie was worth seeing *despite the high ticket price*

   OR *despite the ticket price being high* (despite).

2. Kala went to an action movie _____ (instead of).

3. Kala got popcorn _____ (in spite of).

4. Kala had a soda _____ (as well as).

5. Kala couldn't see the movie very well _____ (due to).

6. Kala's neck hurts _____ (as a result of).

3 Combine the sentences about an animated movie. Use the prepositions in parentheses. Sometimes more than one answer is possible.

1. Let's see an animated movie. I don't want to see an action movie. (instead of)

   Let's see an animated movie instead of an action movie. OR *Let's see*
   an animated movie instead of seeing an action movie.

2. All the movies I own are live action. *Hop* is the only animated movie I have. (except for)

   _____

3. *Hop* is a sweet movie. It's also very funny. (besides)

   _____

4. *Hop* has animated characters in it. It also has "real" actors in it. (in addition to)

_____

5. The main actor talks to other people. He also talks to an animated bunny. (as well as)

_____

4 Write sentences about the topics in parentheses. Use the prepositions in the box or your own ideas. Write sentences that are true for you.

as a result of	besides	except for	instead of
because of	despite	in addition to	

1. (animated movies) _____

2. (action movies) _____

3. (movie ticket prices) _____

4. (movie snacks) _____

5. (mocap technology) _____

6. (renting DVDs) _____

Connecting Information with Transition Words

1 Look at the time line about animated movies. Then write sentences with the simple past and the sequence words in the box. Sometimes more than one answer is possible.

A Quick History of Animated Movies

1832   Joseph Plateau and Simon von Stampfer / invent / machines that showed animated images

1906   J. Stuart Blackton / make / the first animated film by using drawings on a blackboard

1910   Émile Cohl / create / an early animated film, using paper cutouts

1914   Winsor McCay / make / an animated cartoon with 10,000 drawings

1917   The first full-length animated movie / be made / in Argentina / by Quirino Cristiani

1928   Walt Disney / produce / the first animated cartoon with synchronized sound[1]

[1]**synchronized sound:** sound happening at the same time as the pictures

after that	finally	~~first~~	next	second	then

1. _First, Joseph Plateau and Simon von Stampfer invented machines that showed animated images._

2. _____

3. _____

4. _____

5. _____

6. _____

2 Complete the paragraphs about motion capture on smartphones. Circle two transition words that correctly complete each sentence.

Motion capture (mocap) technology is used for many smartphone applications. For example, mocap is used to record people dancing. (Then)/ Thus /(After that), the
(1)
movements are animated. When you use the application on your phone, you watch the animated character in order to learn the dance steps. **In addition / Moreover / Finally**,
(2)
mocap is used for exercise programs. Mocap captures people doing different kinds of exercise moves, which are turned into animation. **Instead / As a result / Consequently**,
(3)
the movements of the characters are realistic. You watch the characters on your phone and follow the exercises. The exercise program is portable when it's on your phone; **therefore / as a result / next**, you can do the exercises anywhere at all in your home.
(4)
Instead / Moreover / Furthermore, you can do them when you travel.
(5)
   In contrast / Thus / On the other hand, some applications actually allow you to
(6)
record images using mocap. You record images easily with your phone's video camera and transfer the data to a computer. One of the uses of this application is for science experiments. For example, you can use mocap to measure movements of a moving object, like a car or an elevator. **In addition / To conclude / Furthermore**, mocap can be used
(7)
to capture movements for animation. You record movements of a person or an object with your phone's video camera.

   On the other hand / To summarize / In conclusion, mocap technology is now used
(8)
in a variety of smartphone apps. If they seem useful to you, get more information on them.

3 Rewrite the sentences about a dance application (app) for a smartphone. Make each sentence into two independent sentences. Replace each word in bold with the correct transition word in parentheses.

1. U-Dance is easy to use, **and** it's a lot of fun. (also / for instance)

   U-Dance is easy to use. Also, it's a lot of fun.

2. Most dance apps only show steps, **but** U-Dance shows a user's movements. (to conclude / in contrast)

   _____

3. I thought the app would not be good exercise, **but** I got a good workout. (however / thus)

   _____

4. U-Dance is free, **so** you have no reason not to get it. (on the other hand / therefore)

   _____

5. **Because** it's easy to use, fun, and free, it's a great app. (to summarize / however)

   _____

Avoid Common Mistakes

1 Circle the mistakes.

1. I like exercising at home **as well as taking classes**. I watch exercise videos
   (a)
   (in addition to I watch yoga videos.) **Despite being hard work**, exercising is fun.
   (b)   (c)

2. My sister and I enjoy TV shows. **In the other hand**, we also enjoy animated movies.
   (a)
   We see many movies at the Great Escapes Theater **as well as the Main Theater**.
   (b)
   Despite its large size, the Main Theater is usually very crowded.
   (c)

3. I bought a mocap application for my phone **as well as software** to make
   (a)
   animation for my computer. I recorded my son **in addition to my daughter**.
   (b)
   In addition to my son has a cute animated character, my daughter's animated
   (c)
   character was also cute.

4. Draw, Inc., uses traditional animation, with drawings by hand. **In contrast**, S&S Design
   (a)
   uses mocap images to animate. Draw, Inc.'s characters have more detail than S&S
   Design's. **In the other hand**, they aren't as realistic. S&S makes movies very quickly.
   (b)
   However, it takes Draw, Inc., a long time to make a movie.
   (c)

5. Roberto likes action movies **in addition to animated movies**. He goes to the movies
   (a)
   on Saturday **as well as he goes on Sunday**. He usually buys popcorn and candy
   (b)
   despite the high price.
   (c)

6. Donna bought complicated animation software. **As a result**, she doesn't know how to
   (a)
   use it. **In the other hand**, the less complicated software didn't have the features she
   (b)
   wanted. **In conclusion**, Donna bought software she can't use.
   (c)

7. **In addition to** the movie, the play *The Phenom Team* has a lot of action and excitement.
   (a)
   In the other hand, the play doesn't have as many special effects. I've seen the movie
   (b)
   as well as the play.
   (c)

8. I'm taking an animation class **in spite of the expense**. **Despite his fast speech**, the
   (a)   (b)
   teacher is very good. He has a good sense of humor **in addition to he has patience**.
   (c)

2 Find and correct five more mistakes in the article about Pixar.

Pixar: A Computer Animation Studio

   Despite ~~it is~~ *being* a relatively young company, Pixar has been very successful. In spite of

he had a good job at Disney, John Lasseter left his job to start a computer animation

company with George Lucas in 1984. The company later became Pixar. In 1986, Pixar

released its first animated short film, which was called *Luxo Jr*. In 1987, *Luxo Jr.* was

5 nominated for an Academy Award as well as it was nominated for a Golden Gate Award.

It won the Golden Gate Award. In the other hand, it did not win the Academy Award. In

1989, Pixar started making commercials in addition to it made films. In the 1990s, Pixar

continued making short films as well as it made commercials. In addition to Pixar's short

films, the commercials also won awards.

10   In 1995, Pixar's *Toy Story* was a huge success at the box office. In addition, it was the

world's first full-length movie completely animated on computers. In the years to come,

Pixar made *Toy Story 2* and *Toy Story 3*. *Toy Story 3* made even more money than the very

successful *Toy Story* and *Toy Story 2* combined. In conclusion, Pixar has had fantastic

success with many of its movies and commercials and has won a large number of awards

15 over the years.

Self-Assessment

Circle the word or phrase that correctly completes each sentence.

1. Animated movies have animated characters _____ actors.

   a. in spite of   b. despite   c. instead of

2. Some movies have animated characters _____ actors.

   a. due to   b. as well as   c. because of

3. _____ using new types of computer animation, moviemakers are making some complex movie projects possible.

   a. As a result of   b. In spite of   c. Except for

4. I don't like any of the *Toy Story* movies _____ the 3D version of *Toy Story 2.*

   a. in spite of   b. because of   c. except for

5. I love going to animated movies _____ all the loud children in the audience.

   a. besides   b. as well as   c. despite

6. _____ Alejandra uses a computer program with mocap for physical therapy.

   a. Instead of using a trainer,   b. Instead using a trainer   c. Using a trainer instead of

7. The success of physical therapy programs that use mocap is _____ the realistic movements of the animation.

   a. in spite of   b. due to   c. besides

8. Paul has had success with his exercise program. _____ trouble being motivated.

   a. Other people   b. However other   c. Other people,
      however have   people have   however, have

9. First, turn on the video camera on your phone. _____ , record a moving image. After that, transfer the data to your computer.

   a. Second   b. Finally   c. Therefore

10. Carl is good at drawing. _____ , he doesn't know much about drawing on computers.

    a. Moreover   b. Instead   c. However

11. Tak-Chung works for a computer animation company; _____ , she is its artistic director.

    a. furthermore   b. on the other hand   c. then

12. Stephanie animated two short films last year. _____ , she animated four commercials.

    a. In conclusion   b. Therefore   c. In addition

13. Pixar has created several animated movies that made a lot of money, and their movies have won several awards. _____ , it's a well-known company.

    a. In contrast   b. Consequently   c. Next

14. Mocap technology is used in exercise videos; _____ , the technology is used in pilot training videos.

    a. first   b. moreover   c. thus

15. Joe's company produces some of the best computer-generated animations. Their work is _____ one of the most expensive.

    a. also   b. in addition   c. though

Art Credits

Illustration

Bill Dickson: 29, 103, 204; **Ortelius Design:** 152; **Rob Schuster:** 11, 127 *(top)*, 195, 196, 202, 210, 221; **Matt Stevens:** 14, 26, 28, 34, 127 *(bottom)*, 128; **Richard Williams:** 19, 20, 186

Photography